Re-Imagining Eve and Adam

Re-Imagining Eve and Adam

And Other Brief Essays

Heidi M. Szpek

Writers Club Press
San Jose New York Lincoln Shanghai

Re-Imagining Eve and Adam
And Other Brief Essays

All Rights Reserved © 2002 by Heidi M. Szpek

No part of this book may be reproduced or transmitted in any form or by any means, graphic, electronic, or mechanical, including photocopying, recording, taping, or by any information storage retrieval system, without the permission in writing from the publisher.

Writers Club Press
an imprint of iUniverse, Inc.

For information address:
iUniverse, Inc.
5220 S. 16th St., Suite 200
Lincoln, NE 68512
www.iuniverse.com

Cover: *The Creation of Eve* (1510) by Fra Bartolommeo.
© The Seattle Art Museum
Gift of the Samuel H. Kress Foundation

Resuscitation of Abel by Father Velghe
& Interior of St. Benedict's Painted Church
Judean Wilderness, Lilith Amulet, Author Photo
© Frank J. Idzikowski

ISBN: 0-595-24906-X

Printed in the United States of America

For my mother,
Dolores Ligman Szpek

Contents

Prelude: On Re-imagining, Essays & Brevity ix

Part I   Re-imagining...

"This is My Beloved and This is My Friend": Re-Imagining Eve
  and Adam 3

"What is This That You Have Done?" 9

What if Adam and Eve Had Been Patient? 15

"In the Image of God He Created Them": Adam and Lilith 19

Part II   Remembering...

About Sarah 29

Sodom and Beyond: Lot and His Daughters 59

Leah of 'Dim' Eyes 69

"Do Not Reject Your Mother's Teaching?!": The Role of Micah's
  Mother in Judges 17 73

Mrs. Job 85

Vashti…Who? 89

Oh, Susanna, Daniel Cried Out for Thee!. 95

Part III   Reclaiming...

The Rape of Dinah: A Quest for Meaning 103

Tamar: Wife, Harlot, Mother............................ 113
The Levite's Concubine: The Story That Never Was 119
Overture: She Walks in Beauty........................... 133
Endnotes 147

Prelude:
On Re-imagining, Essays &
Brevity

On Re-imagining, Essays & Brevity

*"Come with me
and you'll be
in a world of Pure Imagination;
take a look and you'll see into your
Imagination.
We'll begin with a spin
traveling in a world of my creation...*[1]

Imagination—the ability to create in one's mind what is not readily perceived by the senses. This ability may transport one to places that exist, but are yet unexperienced. *'Pure Imagination'*- envisioning, creating what is free from prior human touch, drawing from a sphere beyond the expectations of the known universe. Between imagination and pure imagination dwells re-imagination, taking what has already been envisioned or interpreted, cleansing our mind's eye and returning once again for a new experience, though not as far as the world of 'pure imagination.' The images we want to create this time are of this world, yet 'pure' in the sense of thoughts untainted by past preconceptions.

The world of the Bible—into which we shall travel—has been overlaid with imagination (scholarship might prefer the term interpretation), generation upon generation upon generation of imagining. Through the ages, this procession of imaginings of biblical women, men, places and customs are quite often influenced by past imaginings rather than the phrasing of the text itself. In the essays that follow my ratiocinations will take the reader into this world between imagination and pure imagination into the realm of re-imagination based on the text and less traditional disciplines for inspiration. In the lead essay of this collection, "This is My Beloved and This is My Friend: Re-imagining Eve and Adam," I will ask the reader to strip away past conceptions of Eve and Adam and, through the media of lyrics and Renaissance art, re-imagine Eve and Adam. The three essays that follow this provocative essay will continue to focus on re-imagining the world of Eve. Part One, *Re-Imagining*, will conclude with an equally provocative essay, "In the Image of God He Created Them: Adam and Lilith," which will challenge the propriety of re-imagining. Lilith, Adam's first wife according to Rabbinic legend, is the subject of this re-imagining. Lilith serves as a representative example of questionable re-imagining, as I query, "when we look to myth and legend for the symbols of contemporary society are we free to rewrite these symbols and excise the distasteful aspects because they derive from the non-historical circumstances or we simply choose to ignore them?"

Before we can re-imagine a biblical woman, however, we must remember her. Part Two, *Remembering*, is directed at reacquainting contemporary society with a select group of biblical women who have been forgotten or overshadowed. We will remember Sarah, the first matriarch, known more often by virtue of her association with Abraham; and Leah, first wife of the patriarch, Jacob, often lost in the shadow of her younger sister Rachel, second beloved wife of Jacob. Perhaps "You have heard of the endurance of Job," records the Epistle of James (5:11). What about Mrs. Job? Is not his suffering, her suffering? When Job lost all his possessions and his ten children, did she not suffer the same losses? And then there is Vashti. "Who?" is the familiar response to the woman who is erased by Queen Esther, a prominent biblical figure who supplants Vashti as queen of Persia and saves her people, the Jews, in their exile in Persia. We will remember, too, Susanna, the 'lily' of Babylon, her story is often forgotten because it appears in the Apocrypha—a deutero-canonical collection of 13-14 texts deemed authoritative by Catholic and Orthodox traditions, but not so in Jewish or Protestant circles. In Part Two, *Remembering*, we will also meet Lot's Daughters and Micah's mother, but theirs are characters with whom we may not wish to make acquaintance.

Remembering each of these seven women will allow the reader to become acquainted—or reacquainted—with each, learning of their beauty, their sorrows, their joy and their significance in the biblical narrative. There are, however, tales of biblical women oppressed and violated which many feminists believe challenge the validity of the entire biblical text from a woman's perspective. Why then would we wish to remember them? In Part Three, *Reclaiming*, the narratives of three oppressed women are examined. We learn of the rape of Dinah, only (recorded) daughter of Jacob and Leah, and Tamar, daughter-in-law of Judah, who turns to 'prostitution' to ensure a secure position in her husband's family. We will also conclude with perhaps the most horrific tale of oppression, the rape, murder and dismemberment of the Levite's concubine. The stories of each of these women could have been included in Part Two, *Remembering*, but their horrific and subjugating nature requires more than remembering. These 'texts of terror' need to be reclaimed by questioning their function. Perhaps re-imagining a deeper level of meaning for each woman can reclaim her from abandonment by those who cannot see beyond the image of misogyny and oppression at the surface level of the text. Their voices need not be suppressed.

The genre employed in these re-imaginings, rememberings and reclaimings is predominantly that of the essay. Personal preference sees the genre of essay as the quintessential medium of writing. Its structure is precise (introduction, body, conclusion); its content can be informative, intuitive and personal. Renowned essayist, novelist and poet Cynthia Ozick would no doubt disagree with me. In her essay (article?) *She: Portrait of the Essay as a Warm Body*, Ozick emphatically promotes the 'genuine' essay as what English instructors would label the personal essay. For Ozick

> AN essay is a thing of the imagination. If there is information in an essay, it is by-the-by, and if there is an opinion, one need not trust it for the long run. A genuine essay rarely has an educational, polemical or sociopolitical use; it is the movement of a free mind at play. Though it is written in prose, it is closer in kind to poetry than to any other form. Like a poem, a genuine essay is made of language and character and mood and temperament and pluck and chance.[2]

That an essay is borne of the imagination, contains the personal, and is crafted in poetic prose, I would most assuredly agree. But an essay need not be void of information or educational value. It can be polemic and/or aphoristic because this genre of writing permits the joining of personal thoughts with 'information.' Of Ozick's 'language and character and mood and temperament and pluck and chance,' it is chance, more precisely chance discoveries that unexpectedly concur with research at hand, that brings exhilaration to the essay. Such discoveries are the source of addendums to and asides in a number of essays inspired by the unexpected: a Sunday afternoon family outing to the Seattle Art Museum for an exhibit on the Discoveries of Sichuan, China adds a dimension to Eve; a disruptive participant in a lecture at the Jewish Community Center of Tucson reveals Lilith is still a powerful force; turning on the television for Live with Regis and Vashti!; the discovery of a rare Rembrandt etching; and finding Eve while in search of King Kamemameha on the Big Island of Hawaii . These discoveries along with the inclusion of the powerful reflections composed by Lauren Deitch, Stan Holland and Betty Lieberman, participants from my adult education series, added 'pluck' to my Re-imaginings, Rememberings and Reclaimings, giving rise to the wondrous potential for further speculation and enlightenment. Within this collection of essays[3] are also three entries,[4] which more properly might be termed articles or papers. The reader will readily discern the more formal nature of these inclusions. Though academically presented, my predilection for the poetic still pervades, and the significance of remembering these women is well worth the lengthier exposition.

Finally, this Preface is entitled "On Re-Imagining, Essays & Brevity." Thus far I have explained the first two elements, but what of brevity—clearly a number of essays are not brief. In the 17th century, the French philosopher and mathematician Pascal wrote, "The present letter is a very long one, simply because I had no leisure to make it shorter."[5] Unlike Pascal, I have tried to make these essays 'short' not because I have leisure, but because loquaciousness does not necessarily guarantee meaningful thought. Rather a poignant succinct essay delivers a powerful message by virtue of brevity for brevity requires precise word choice. And so whenever possible I extend to you my reader a silver tray with a few delectable morsels, rather than a cup that overfloweth, for in this way you may savor each tidbit and decide for yourself what is a delectable *Re-imagining*, a desired *Remembering* or a palatable *Reclaiming*.

PART I
Re-imagining...

○ ○
"Grow old with me/the best is yet to be!"
—Robert Browning

"This is My Beloved and This is My Friend": Re-Imagining Eve and Adam

"His locks are wavy, black as the raven. His eyes are like doves, beside springs of water, bathed in milk, fitly set... This is my beloved and this is my friend," sings Eve. Eve! *"Behold, you are beautiful my love. Behold you are beautiful, your eyes are doves; Behold, you are beautiful my beloved. Truly lovely!"* rejoins Adam. Adam! These words, drawn from the love poetry of the biblical text of the Song of Songs, adapted and set to music by award-winning playwright Elizabeth Swados in the Broadway musical *Bible Women*,[6] ask us, implore us, sway us through their passionate melodious invocations to consider Eve and Adam as 'beloveds and friends.' But can we envision them as such, openly singing of their devotion to one another?

While many contemporary interpretations view their story as a myth explaining the origin of humankind, sin, mortality, and gender roles, ancient and medieval interpretations were often unable to move beyond the literal level. With one bite of 'the apple,' Eve brought sin, human mortality, expulsion from Paradise, and woman's sub-ordinance into the world. In one Ancient Jewish tradition, Eve is depicted as a manipulator:

> *Scarce had she finished, when she saw the Angel of Death before her. Expecting her end to come immediately she resolved to make Adam eat of the forbidden fruit, too, lest he espouse another wife after her death.*

> *It required tears and lamentations on her part to prevail upon Adam to take the baleful step. Not yet satisfied, she gave of the fruit to all other living beings, that they, too, might be subject to death.*[7]

Reread Genesis 3:6 "…she took of its fruit and ate; and she also gave some to her husband, who was with her, and he ate." The text says nothing about tears, lamentations or giving fruit to all other living beings. In the New Testament the guilt of Eve is passed on to all women. In 1 Timothy 2:12-14, Paul writes:

> *I permit no woman to teach or have authority over a man; she is to keep silent. For Adam was formed first, then Eve; and Adam was deceived, but the woman was deceived and became a transgressor. Yet she will be saved through childbearing, provided they continue in faith and love and holiness with modesty.*

Eve, the deceptive transgressor, is not confined to ancient literature. John Milton (1608-1674) closes his poem *Paradise Lost* with the classic lines (Book IX:1182-1186):

> *Thus it shall befall*
>
> *Him who, to worth in women overtrusting,*
>
> *Lets her rule; restraint she will not brook,*
>
> *And, left to herself, if evil thence ensue,*
>
> *She first his weak indulgence will accuse.*[8]

Who blamed whom? The text of Genesis 3:12-13 reads, "the man said, 'the woman whom you gave to be with me, she gave me fruit from the tree, and I ate.' The woman said, 'The serpent tricked me, and I ate'." Adam blamed woman and *God*; Eve admitted being tricked. Eve did *not* blame Adam.

Interpretations such as these have forced us to view the story of Eve and Adam as a tragedy, not a love story. How then can we re-imagine

Eve and Adam as "beloveds and friends?" In the biblical text they do not exchange a single word; all dialogue is between God and Adam, God and Eve or the serpent and Eve. Their relationship is revealed through their actions as told by the narrator of Genesis 2-4. We cannot ignore their actions as disobedient; their punishments provide the explanation for the human condition. We can, however, re-imagine Eve and Adam by noting the obvious—Eve and Adam had a relationship. We overlook this detail because we were taught to focus on the mythic nature or tragedy of their story—sin brings mortality and a lost paradise. We can and should not ignore these details, but if we consider these events as part of the development in their relationship, we can re-imagine Eve and Adam in a more positive light. We can add a new dimension to Eve and Adam that will enrich their significance and value. They were part of a relationship that developed and changed throughout the course of the most overwhelming events, and this relationship *endured*.

Having erred, Eve and Adam are held accountable for their actions. It is significant, too, that Adam finally names the woman, Eve, meaning '(mother of all) living,' *after* they are disobedient (Gen. 3:20). Scholars often overlook this detail. Had Adam bore any anger against Eve, would he bestow upon her the gift of a name? They persevere, continue. They do not dissolve their relationship even in the face of another adversity—expulsion from the Garden. Joy follows sorrow with the birth of two sons, Cain and Abel. Sorrow follows this joy when the elder Cain murders the younger Abel out of jealousy (Genesis 4); fratricide has shattered their life. As "beloveds and friends" they do not separate from each other at a time of immense tragedy, rather they turn to each other. They not only lose Abel, but Cain is separated from his parents when God punishes him to be "a fugitive and wanderer on the earth" (Genesis 4:12). Joy again follows sorrow: "Adam knew his wife again, and she bore a son and named him Seth" (Genesis 4:25). The birth of another child can never replace the loss of one, but Seth's birth suggests that Adam and Eve sought solace with each other.

The biblical text does not explicitly continue the story of Eve and Adam. However, tucked away in the genealogy of Adam (Genesis 5:1-5) we read, "the days of Adam after he became the father of Seth were eight hundred years; *and he had other sons and daughters.*"⁹ Our attention in the biblical text may be directed toward the next major story, Noah and the Flood, but the presence of this oft-forgotten line reminds us that the story of Eve and Adam did go on. It may not contain the drama of their earlier years, but the birth of other sons and daughters tells us their relationship continued to mature *and it endured.*

The assumption of 'a relationship' lies behind Swados' connection of Adam and Eve with the Song of Songs. Swados' Eve sings three songs adapted from the Song of Songs, chronicling the maturation of Eve's love for Adam.

This first song of Eve, adapted from Song of Songs 2:8-16, is sung in a playful, giddy manner.

> *The voice of my beloved,*
> *Behold he comes.*
> *Leaping up on mountains,*
> *Bounding over the hills.*
> *My beloved is like a gazelle,*
> *or a young stag.*
> *Behold, there he stands behind our wall,*
> *gazing in at the windows, looking through the lattice,*
> *my beloved speaks, and says to me, and says to me—Arise my beloved!*

Lyrics and melody burst with excitement at Eve's first recognition of her love for Adam, not physical desire, but that pure emotional tugging of one's heartstrings toward another human being. Eve goes on to sing a much more intense song, a song that indicates her love has gone beyond that giddy phase of this first song. Her second song, *"My Beloved is All Radiant and Ruddy,"* is once again drawn from Song of Songs (5:9-16). Melody and words project us into a surreal world, a world like the idyllic oasis garden, before temptation. Eve's love for

Adam is growing and maturing, both emotionally and physically. Her voice rises in a crescendo *"his appearance is like Lebanon,"* then falls softly away *"this is my beloved and this is my friend."* When we consider what follows in Genesis 3—the temptation, eating of the fruit, punishments and banishment from the Garden—it is perhaps this dual role of beloved and friend that gives Eve and Adam the strength to endure.

Eve's final song, *"Arise My Beloved, My Fair One,"* drawn from Song of Songs 2:10-16, is slow, contemplative. Their relationship has moved to a new level. Adam and Eve have both eaten of the fruit and discovered the realities of life. Eve beckons Adam to depart from their old garden paradise: *"Arise my beloved, my fair one and come away,"* culminating in the refrain *"my beloved is mine and I am his, my beloved is mine and I am his."*

Adam responds in song, adapted from Song of Songs 4. He acknowledges her beauty and his love *"Behold, you are beautiful my love...Your eyes are like doves, you are beautiful my beloved, truly lovely, truly lovely."* Together they sing *"Behold you are beautiful my love,...my beloved."* Adam intones, *"You are lovely, truly lovely, truly lovely"* and in unison they sing *"truly lovely, truly lovely."* Moving out into the world, their relationship is one of interdependence, respect and love.

◆ ◆ ◆

In the Medieval and Renaissance Gallery of the Seattle Art Museum hangs the Renaissance painting *The Creation of Eve*, c. 1510, by the Dominican friar Fra. Bartolommeo (Italian, 1472-1517) [cover photo]. Foreground, left, in a soft green paradisal setting stands God, garbed in a regal red robe. His right hand is extended toward Eve whose outstretched fingertips ever so gently touch the fingertips of God, as she emerges naked from the left side of Adam who reposes on the garden's grassy floor. In the background—reduced in size—are enjoined in familial play, a woman, a man and two very small boys. It is the foreground scene, however, that first captures the viewer's attention. The impact is not only due to the action of Eve literally emerging out of Adam's side, but the delicacy of her hand extended toward her Creator—and her Creator reciprocates.

To the left of this painting the placard reads, *The Creation of Eve* "emphasizes [the] closeness of Adam and Eve by showing the moment when God creates Eve from Adam's 'rib.' Renaissance artists developed a more positive view, concentrating on the brief period before the Fall of Man, when human existence was full of promise." What is this promise? The discerning eye is drawn from foreground to background as the viewer comes to realize that the familial group is that of Eve, Adam and their twin sons, Cain and Abel. Much has transpired in the biblical narrative between the events of the foreground and the background, but Bartolommeo paints no hue of disobedience or tragedy. His painting delivers the message of Creation of humankind directly linked to God, and these same creations, Adam and Eve, bound with new creation as evinced by the presence of their two small boys.

Fra. Bartolommeo presented to his Renaissance audience a new vision of the world in his *The Creation of Eve*. Visually he challenged them to refocus their preconception of Eve as the 'mother' of all woes and her story as one of tragedy borne out of misconduct. Focus is on Creation with its closeness to God and the ensuing family. Swados presents us with this same challenge, this time through the medium of her music and lyrical adaptations. Both artists—five hundred years apart—implore us to re-imagine this story not as tragedy, but as a paradigm of the first relationship depicting the trials and tribulations of a man and woman, the realities of their life, and the understanding that interdependence will allow their relationship to continue and to endure. Re-imagine Adam and Eve as the first model of what a true committed relationship entails: 'beloveds and friends.'

"What is This That You Have Done?"

"What is this that you have done?" Sadly these are the first words God speaks to Eve. Eve responds, "the serpent tricked me, and I ate" (Genesis 3:13). Eve had eaten of the forbidden fruit: "she took of its fruit and ate" (Genesis 3:6). For this transgression Eve is punished. God's last and only other words to Eve are "I will greatly increase your toil and childbirths, along with toil you shall bring forth children; yet your desire shall be for your husband and he shall rule over you" (Genesis 3:16). God comes down hard on Eve, but compared to Western Civilization God is merciful. Eve is deemed responsible for thb loss of paradise, mankind's mortality, the presence of sin and by extension the subordination of all women. But what of Adam? Were his actions beyond reproach? If we look closer at the events of Genesis 3 we might wish to reconsider whom—if anyone—should be blamed for the human condition.

In Genesis 3 we have a paradise garden, well watered with delectable food, a man and woman presumably content in their existence, 'a forbidden tree' and a cunning serpent. The storyline is familiar to most readers; its outcome is predictable. We the reader were told at the beginning of this episode that the serpent was "the most crafty of all living creatures" (Gen. 3:1). We as readers should be prepared for an exhibition of his craftiness. And indeed we witness it in the tricking of Eve. Feigning ignorance the serpent asks her if God said, "Shall you not eat from any tree in the garden?" (Gen. 3:1) The woman eagerly responds—Oh no! Only that one tree in the middle of the garden—adding that we may not even touch it! (Gen. 3:3). The cunning serpent tells her this is not true, rather God forbids them to eat of its fruit because then they will become like God, knowing good and evil! (Gen. 3:4-5). The woman succumbs to the temptation: "She took of its fruit and ate and she also gave some to her husband, who was with her, and he ate" (Gen. 3:6). No one forced the woman *or* the man; they both chose freely. What follows next in our story is the most misrepresented scene in this episode.

Our setting is still the oasis paradise, but now the man and woman, aware of their nakedness, are clothed—symbolic of their lost innocence. They hide from God (Gen. 3:7-8). In a very personal dialogue, God questions first the man, then the woman.

> *But the Lord God called to the man, and said to him, 'Where are you?'*
>
> *He said, 'I heard the sound of your voice in the garden, and I was afraid, because I was naked; and I hid myself.'*
>
> *He [God] said, 'Who told you that you were naked? Have you eaten from the tree of which I commanded you not to eat?'*
>
> *The man said, 'The woman whom you gave to be with me, she gave me fruit from the tree, and I ate.'*
>
> *Then the Lord God said to the woman, 'What is this that you have done?'*
>
> *The woman said, 'The serpent tricked me, and I ate.'* (Gen. 3:9-13)

The interplay between man, woman and God is spectacular. God knows very well where Man is, yet he calls out to him as any father would to a son playing in his backyard. When Man admits he was afraid because he was naked, he is admitting, like a child, he has done something wrong. God poses the stern questions, "Who told you you were naked? Have you eaten of the tree of which I commanded you not to eat?" (Gen. 3:11). The man responds to neither question. Rather what follows may be the prototype of the classic 'pass the buck' scene. The man points a finger at the woman: "The woman whom you gave to be with me, she gave me fruit from the tree, and I ate." Man is not only passing the buck to the woman—'the woman she gave me fruit,' but he has also passed the buck to God, slyly reminding God that it was "The woman whom YOU [God] gave to be with me, she gave me fruit from the tree, and I ate." Man's statement ends with "and I ate," not 'and she forced me or tricked me to eat,' but "*I* ate." Recall, too, that in Genesis 3:6 the text reads, "she took of its fruit and ate; and she also gave some to her husband, WHO WAS WITH HER, AND HE ATE." It is crucial for the reader to know that the biblical text clearly indicates that Man was with Woman when she ate. That he was oblivious to what she was doing seems hard to accept. After acknowledging his presence, the text simply states "and he ate," there is no suggestion that he was forced or tricked into partaking of the fruit. However, when called to account for his actions Man tries to divert the truth, focusing the guilt on Woman and on God, Creator of Woman.

The ancient Jewish historian Josephus (1st CE) as well as Rabbinic literature noted that Adam shifted the blame.[10] In the seventeenth century, John Milton's classic *Paradise Lost* took this position to the extreme.[11] Milton relates that Eve suggested to Adam that they separate from each other to attend to the growing demands of tending the Garden (Book IX, 202-209). Eve and Adam separate. Their separation is crucial because Eve is alone and vulnerable to the snake's temptation. Alone she succumbs to temptation (Book IX, 780-784). After greedily satiating herself with the forbidden fruit, she now believes all wisdom is open to her. Eve resolves that "in bliss or woe" Adam shall share with her all the wonders of knowledge (Book IX, 830-831). When Adam is told, his reaction is quite unlike that of the biblical version:

> Adam, as soon as he heard
> The fatal trespass done by Eve, amazed,
> Astonied stood and blank, while horror chill

Ran through his veins, and all his joints relaxed. (Book IX, 888-891)

Adam eats of the forbidden fruit, certain that he will die. But no matter, for without Eve he cannot envision life:

> How can I live without thee, how forgo
> Thy sweet converse and love so dearly joined,
> To live again in these wild woods forlorn?
> Should God create another Eve, and I
> Another rib afford, yet loss of thee
> Would never from my heart; no, no! (Book IX, 908-913).

Milton may have exaggerated Woman's cunning, but that biblical Woman, too, tried to 'pass the buck' cannot be denied.

To Woman God says, "What is this that you have done?" (Gen. 3:13). Passing the buck, she responds, "The serpent tricked me, and I ate" (Gen. 3:13). Like the man, she admits that she ate the fruit. The simple statement, "and I ate" is present in both their confessions. Like the man, she takes the blame from her shoulders and places it on another's—the serpent's. But Eve specifically states, "He tricked me," as if her guilt should be deemed less because her action was carried out under this guise of deception. The ancient Jewish philosopher Philo (1st CE) noted that the serpent did not physically *give* her the fruit, but he *beguiled* or *tricked* her into experiencing the pleasure of the fruit.[12] Philo saw Eve as a victim rather than a criminal. We, too, might try to vindicate Woman by saying that when the ban on eating the fruit was introduced (Gen. 2:17), the woman was not yet created; however, in Genesis 3:2-3 she clearly has become aware of it when she added, "nor shall you touch it." Eve, however, does deserve commendation for the extent to which she 'passes the buck.' Like Man she may be 'passing the buck' to the serpent, yet she does tell the truth. She does not say, "the serpent whom you [God] created, tricked me and I ate." She does not 'pass the buck' to God.

Ultimately then, whose behavior is more reprehensible? Who is to blame for the loss of paradise? Both have erred. Both have avoided taking complete responsibility for their actions. We as readers might feel that we can shift or lessen the blame depending on how we intone their confessions, or which words we choose to emphasize. But how the original must be intoned is not preserved in the oldest extant manuscripts of the Hebrew Bible. The system of accentuation dates to a much later period.[13] Thus, we must let the words speak for themselves. Consider their words once more: (Man) "The woman whom you gave to be with me, she gave me fruit from the tree, and I ate"; (Woman) "The serpent tricked me, and I ate." Both Man and Woman confess, "I ate." The statement before this confession is the crux of the issue. Both are technically telling the truth. It is true that "the woman whom you [God] gave to be with me, she gave me fruit from the tree." God did indeed create Woman and Woman gave Man the fruit. It is also true that 'the serpent tricked me [Eve]. However, whose 'truth' is more reprehensible, a man who blames Woman and God, or a Woman who blames her folly? How we answer this question determines where we place the blame or if we need to place blame for the human condition.

What if Adam and Eve Had Been Patient?

What if the Allies had lost D-day? What if the South had won the Civil War? What if Alexander the Great had not died at the age of 33? 'What if' is a popular exercise for imagining that if an event had happened differently, the world would be a different place, perhaps better, perhaps worse. The Bible is not immune to these 'what if' scenarios, with the Garden of Eden story the most popular story to re-imagine. What if Eve had not eaten of the fruit? What if Adam had said no to Eve? What if there was never a serpent? Would the world be a better place? Would evil, sickness and every imaginable horror of the human condition not exist? Most attempts to answer these 'what ifs' suggest that the world would indeed be a Paradise had Adam and Eve been obedient.

Harold Kushner in *How Good Do We Have to Be? A New Understanding of Guilt and Forgiveness,* however, provides us with an alternate outcome when Adam and Eve do NOT eat of the fruit:[14]

> *So the woman saw that the tree was good to eat and a delight to the eye, and the serpent said to her, 'Eat of it, for when you eat of it, you will be as wise as God.' But the woman said, 'No, God has commanded us not to eat of it, and I will not disobey God.'*
>
> *And God called to the man and the woman and said to them, 'Because you have hearkened to My word and not disobeyed My command, I shall reward you greatly.' To the man, He said, 'You will never have to work again. Spend all your days in idle contentment, with food growing all around you.' To the woman, He said, 'You will bear children without pain and you will raise them without pain.*

They will need nothing from you. Children will not cry when their parents die, and parents will not cry when their parents die.' To both of them, He said, 'For the rest of your lives, you will have full bellies and contented smiles. You will never cry and you will never laugh. You will never long for something you don't have, and you will never receive something you always wanted.' And the man and the woman grew old together in the garden, eating daily from the Tree of Life and having many children. And the grass grew high around the Tree of Knowledge of Good and Evil until it disappeared from view, for there was no one to tend it.

Humankind is obedient, they are fruitful and multiply, but they are stagnant, without challenges, without emotions. Has obedience brought a better world?

Another 'what if' scenario allows us to maintain the biblical story, but suggests that 'what if' God had predetermined the flow of history and the events in the Garden were part of His plan. Stan Holland voiced this view when he composed this 'what if' for a bible studies course at Congregation Emmanuel B'ne Jeshurun in Milwaukee, WI:[15]

What if the fruit had not been eaten? Would Adam and Eve still be living in Eden? Certainly God's knowledge of the nature of man would make Adam's action predictable. God, placing the tree in the center of the garden and issuing the prohibition to eat of it, would seem to indicate a decision of God to terminate the original relationship and replace it with a new one in which man and God become partners. Man could then be obedient or defiant—free to grow toward or away from God. Man can never achieve godlike status or power; nevertheless, by choosing knowledge with mortality, man has attained a measure of freedom to control his own destiny.

Since God is omniscient, He knew that man would act, not only did He know but He desired man to take the initiative so that God and man could have a new relationship. Mankind could have some 'control of his own destiny' while still fulfilling God's command in Genesis

1:28: "God blessed them [man and woman], and said to them, 'Be fruitful and multiply, and fill the earth and subdue it."

Holland's view of the omniscient God is likewise present in a variant 'what if' once again by Kushner. He suggests, "that the story of the Garden of Eden is a tale, not of Paradise Lost but of Paradise outgrown, not of Original Sin but of the Birth of Conscience."[16] It "is a mythical description of how the first human beings left the world of animal existence behind and entered the problematic world of being human."[17] He suggests that when God told Adam not to eat of the fruit, it was not "just a prohibition but a warning."[18] God may have wanted them to eat of the fruit, "though He knew it would make their lives painful and complicated and He winced at the pain they would be condemning themselves to, because God didn't want to be the only One in the world who knew the difference between Good and Evil."[19] Both Holland and Kushner do not ask us to imagine 'what if' the events did not happen, but 'what if' this was God's plan for giving man free will and allowing civilization to flourish. Both work within the confines of the biblical story. Mankind could be a part of his own destiny, but this involvement would bring its share of pain, 'pain' that would allow man to choose to grow or be stagnant.

In the majority of 'what if' scenarios proposed, one scenario is ignored. 'What if' mankind did not take the initiative? Must the outcome be that mankind would not advance? Is it so improbable that the God of the Hebrew Bible, who systematically created the universe and created mankind in His own image (Gen. 1:26-27), might not have a few ideas of His own? The story we now have and its interpretations through the ages, both in the academy and in everyday converse, were borne of humankind's disobedient initiative—this cannot be denied. Is humankind, however, so arrogant to presume that history could only unfold if Adam and Eve took the initiative? WHAT IF humankind had been patient?

"In the Image of God He Created Them": Adam and Lilith

Before Eve there was Lilith. "And when the Holy One Blessed Be He created Adam, the first [man] was the only one. He said 'It is not good for the man to be by himself.' So He created for him a woman from the man like him and He called her Lilith," records Rabbinic legend of the 10th-11th CE in a text known as the *Alphabet of Ben Sira*. This is not the first reference to Lilith for her history spans nearly 5000 years. Today she is still present, embraced in some circles as the first feminist and esteemed as the symbol of modern feminism.

In Ancient Mesopotamia (2400BC), Lilith was viewed as a seductress and a vampire, the antithesis of a good wife. She was equated with Lilitu, a she-demon, one of four demons that belonged to the vampire class. Lilith also appears in the ancient Mesopotamian text, "Gilgamesh and the Huluppu Tree," where she is called "a beautiful maiden," a euphemism for a harlot and vampire. Once she chose a lover, she would never let him go. This Lilith was unable to bear children.[20]

In the Hebrew Bible, Lilith's existence is inferred from Genesis 1:27: "So God created humankind in his image, in the image of God he created them; *male and female* He created them." This 'female' was not formed from Adam's rib as Eve was in Genesis 2, thus this 'female' must be another wife of Adam, *or so reasoned the Rabbis.*[21] The term Lilith is mentioned only once in the biblical text (Isaiah 34:14): "Wildcats shall meet with hyenas, goat-demons shall call to each other; there too *lilith* shall repose."[22] Isaiah was referring to the kingdom of Edom in this verse, an utterly desolate land, which twice refused aid to the Israelites when they were attacked by the Babylonians in the 6th century BC. This is the country where '*lilith*' reposes.

The most fully developed account of the legend of Lilith is found in a controversial medieval text known as the *Alphabet of Ben Sira*. The author of the *Alphabet* attributed his work to the wise Ben Sira (c. 186BC), and involved Ben Sira in the legends to add credibility to his work.[23]

The Alphabet begins with an alphabetically arranged series of not-so-witty, male-oriented, misogynist proverbs.[24] After these proverbs Ben Sira is quizzed seven times about his knowledge of the Bible and Rabbinic literature. His wisdom is acknowledged by 'The Teacher' and his fame becomes so great that word of him reaches King Nebuchadnezzar of Babylon (albeit historically inaccurate because Nebuchadnezzar lived about four hundred years before Ben Sira). During the course of Ben Sira's testing, the king's son becomes ill. Nebuchadnezzar demands that his son be healed through the wisdom of Ben Sira or Ben Sira would suffer the fate of death. An amulet, inscribed with the names of three angels, is prepared for the child. At this point the legend of Lilith unfolds to explain the significance of the amulet.

The legend relates that a woman named Lilith, like Adam, was created from the earth. They quarreled over who should be in the top position during sexual relations. Lilith, claiming her equality, would not lie below Adam. Pronouncing the Ineffable Name of God,[25] she flew off to the Reed (Red) Sea. Three angels tried to convince her to return, but she would not. Her punishment was meted out: one hundred of her children would die every day, children who were born from her promiscuity with demons at the Reed Sea. Lilith, thus, took on the role of a woman who preyed on newborn infants. An amulet inscribed with the names of the three angels was the only way to ward off her evil effects.

In the course of this legend we learn that Lilith was a woman who was created equal, demanded her equality, was refused her equality and then suffered the consequences of her defiance of male authority. On not achieving equality, she was transformed into the antithesis of a good mother, a creature who preys on children.

Lilith, however, was not forgotten. In later Jewish mystical literature of the Kabbalah (especially in the Zohar), Lilith as seductress is further developed.[26] Lilith would entice men in their sleep, gathering semen from nocturnal emissions and even collecting semen from the marriage bed. In this way she became pregnant, bearing numerous demonic children. In the Kabbalah, Lilith would go on to take a husband, the demon Samael, and later divide into Lilith the Elder and Lilith the Younger. She would become the counterpart of the good female divine presence, the Shekinah.[27]

In contemporary literature, Lilith, as seductress *par excellance,* is present in the poetry of Robert Browning,[28] developed by modern Israeli writers S.Y. Agnon, Amos Oz, and A.B. Yehoshua and by western writers George MacDonald and J.R. Salamanca. Salamanca's novel *Lilith* (1961) was later turned into a screenplay (1964). Lilith came to represent the menacing figure that reveals man's fear of woman; the creature who leads him astray.[29]

Throughout the ages Lilith was depicted in a variety of ways: on an ancient terra-cotta relief from Mesopotamia (c. 2000BC) she is given a female form, wings (so she can fly as in our legend), and owl feet indicating she is a creature of the night. She stands atop two lions flanked by owls, indicating both her power over the strongest of beasts and that she herself is a creature of the night. Her hands are raised, each holding a combined ring and rod.[30] Likewise from Arslan Tash in Upper Syria were found in 1933 two limestone plaques. One bears the outline of two reclining creatures resembling she-wolfs, one with wings and a scorpion's tale, one swallowing a small figure. An excerpt from the incantation reads:

> ...The house I enter, you shall not enter,
> and the courtyard I tread, you shall not tread...
> Against the flying ones: from the dark chamber
> Pass now, now, night demons,
> From the house begone outside...[31]

A hole at the top of this plaque suggests it was probably hung within a home, attesting to the belief in the powers of Lilith.

Lilith is also depicted on incantation bowls from Babylonia (sixth century AD). Within these bowls are inscribed magical texts to ward off Lilith or aid in removing her. Scholars suggest that the bowls may have been filled with water or wine, which the bewitched drank; the efficacy of the incantation was thus achieved with the drinking of the liquid. The bowls may also have been used to trap the evil spirits, for some were found overturned in the corners of houses.[32] Like the ancient Egyptian Execration texts the bowls may also have been smashed to achieve efficacy of the incantation.[33] From the 18th CE is also preserved a Persian amulet with figure of Lilith is rough outline, the inscription below reads, "Protect this newborn child from all harm."[34]

Contemporary times have viewed Lilith in a new light. Sarah McCaughlin's *Lilith Fair* (late 90s) promoted Lilith as the feminine ideal of independence, equality and women's achievements as exhibited in music. Today, too, the popular Jewish women's magazine *Lilith* embraces Lilith as the model of womanhood and possibly the first feminist. *Lilith* magazine's editorial page does provide her textual provenance, citing however, a paraphrase and excerpt of those tantalizing first lines of *The Alphabet of Ben Sira*, attractively set beside a *pear*: "In the Garden of Eden, long before the eating of the apple...The Holy One created the first human beings -- a man, Adam, and a woman,

Lilith. Lilith said, 'We are equal because we are created from the same earth'."

Consider Lilith's history. Do we want to emulate a literary figure borne out of medieval misogyny, a character developed as a harsh parody of the so-called folly and danger of women? Should we look no further than her initial demand for equality and ignore the rest of her development? Moreover, can we separate this Lilith from the earlier demonic portrayals of Lilith from Mesopotamia? Can we separate this Lilith from the later Rabbinic and literary developments of Lilith as the antithesis of mother and wife? Can or should we embrace her as the first feminist or adopt her as a symbol for modern feminists? When we look to myth or legend for the symbols of contemporary society are we free to rewrite these symbols and excise the distasteful aspects because they derive from non-historical circumstances or we simply choose to ignore them? Consider the full text of Lilith as found in the *Alphabet of Ben Sira* and decide if Lilith belongs to the domain of *Re-imagining*:

> *"And when the Holy One Blessed Be He created Adam, the first [man] was the only one. He said 'It is not good for the man to be by himself.' So He created for him a woman from the earth like him and He called her Lilith. Immediately they began to quarrel (or: became impassionate) with each other. She said, "I will not lie below." And he said, "I will not lie below, but above, because you are fit for below and I for above." She said to him, "We are both equal because we both come from the earth." But they would not listen to one another. As soon as Lilith saw [this], she said The Ineffable Name [of God] and flew off into the air of the world.*
>
> *Adam stood in prayer before his Creator and said, "O Master of the World, the woman whom you gave to me, has fled from me." Immediately, the Holy One Blessed Be He sent three messengers after her to bring her back. The Holy One Blessed Be He said, "If she wants to come back, fine! But if not she must permit one hundred of her children to die every day."*
>
> *They [the angels] left God and went after her and found her in the midst of the sea in the terrible waters in which the Egyptians were destined to die and they told her God's word. But she did not want to*

return. The angels said to her, "We shall drown you in the sea!" She said to them, "Leave me alone, for I was created only to cause illness to infants. If he is male, I have dominion over him from the day in which he is born until he is eight days old; and if female until she is twenty days old."

When they heard her words, they insisted she be taken back. But she swore to them by the name of the living and eternal God [and said], "Every time that I see you or your names or your images on an amulet, I will not have dominion over the infant." And she agreed that one hundred of her children would die every day. Therefore, every day one hundred of the demons die. Likewise we write their names [the angels'] on an amulet for young children, for when she sees them, she remembers the oath and the child is healed.[35]

◆   ◆   ◆

One summer's eve in 1998, respite from the oppressive heat of the Sonoran desert, which cradled Tucson, Arizona, was found within the cool confines of the Jewish Community Center. Each Wednesday evening that summer a group of mostly women and myself had been gathering for lecture and discussion in connection with the adult education program *Bible Women: Ancient Images and New Perspectives*.[36] We had progressed from a general introduction, to discussions on Vashti, Esther, Ruth, Miriam, and Sarah. Tonight was Lilith's night. The usual crowd gathered, save one. While checking my roster at the registration desk, a stocky, elderly Israeli gentleman inquired where the Lilith lecture was being held and who the instructor was. In response, I turned and introduced myself. His response was demeaning: "YOU are teaching about Lilith?!" He said no more. Heading down the hallway to our meeting room, I was followed slowly, laboriously by this newest participant. His speech, though brief, revealed linguistic ties to Israel and Eastern Europe; his measured, conscious walk suggested a past life of physical hardship. Instinct told me an atmosphere of ease would not pervade tonight's lecture and discussion.

Materials were distributed and the lecture was about to begin, or so I thought. Scarce had a word of introduction emerged from my lips when he interrupted, "Did I know Lilith was mentioned here…Lilith appeared here…You didn't say Lilith is also mentioned in Job!" Politely I responded that, if permitted, I would be addressing the texts to which he referred. When verbal interruption ceased, he persisted rustling through the handouts on Lilith, examining photos, sketches and texts. Repeatedly he turned those papers. The rustling of papers was audible enough to disrupt the lecture; that the other participants were unsettled was evident. Each interruption, each rustle of a page, brought the temperature of our indoor refuge closer to that of the intense Sonoran desert. As the temperature rose, so did my ire until finally, mid-sentence, I asked him to stop. He did not react; he just continued to turn those pages one…after…another, in search of something. This 'gentleman' was not interested in what I had to say regarding Lilith's ancient, biblical, rabbinic, or literary history. Neither the lyrics nor music of Elizabeth Swados' *Lilith* composition, nor our questioning of Lilith as a feminist role model sparked any response. One statement on my part, however, with a question from a hesitant participant, revealed why he was present on this evening. The amulets.

The legend of Lilith spoke of an amulet that would protect the bearer, in particular young children; Middle Eastern discoveries as recent as the 18th century revealed that this legend was not just superstition. My hesitant participant shared that she had heard of such amulets still existing. "Could this be true?" she quizzed. I never had a chance to respond, for my 'gentleman' took the question. He had a passion for collecting Lilith amulets. Exploring bazaars of the Middle East and shops throughout Eastern Europe he had acquired many amulets, dating not just to antiquity or the 18th century, but also to the present day. How many did he possess? "Many," was the curt response. "How did they look? How had he found them? How much had they cost? How were they used? Why did he collect them?" In spite of his intimidating, disruptive nature he now intrigued us. Whether or not desired, he had our attention. We were ready and willing to listen. But no answers were forthcoming! He shrugged off our questions. The hour struck nine—the time for closing our gathering; he rose abruptly. Aided by his cane he exited the room, paying no heed to the cautious good nights from those within.

He did not return the next week or any other weeks. Why he came at all I cannot be sure. Clearly his interest was in Lilith, but what I or other participants had to share was not what he sought. Of what he possessed of Lilith, the amulets, he but tantalized us and left. Despite his unsettling presence, his predilection for collecting 'Liliths' taught me that in some quarters of the contemporary world Lilith is more than legend. To this day when I chance upon a young woman sporting a Lilith tee shirt, I can't help but remember that hot summer night in Tucson and the message of its peculiar visitor. And I wonder whether this young woman truly understands what Lilith represents.

Lilith Amulet (Acquired by author 2002)

PART II
Remembering…

ooooooooooooooooooooooooooo
"Remember me when I am gone away…
Yet if you should forget me for a while
And afterwards remember, do not grieve…
Better by far you should forget and smile
Than that you should remember and be sad."

—*Christina Rossetti*

About Sarah

"In the beginning God created the heavens and the earth" (Gen. 1:1). Then came Adam and Eve, Cain and Abel, angels mating with women, Noah and the flood, a naked, drunken Noah (a story depicting the prominence of his son Shem as the eponymous ancestor of the Semites), and the Tower of Babel. This is the Primeval History, Gen. 1-11. But the story goes on! At the end of chapter 11, from what appears to be a tedious genealogy of more unknowns than knowns, a certain Terah emerges from the lineage of Shem. Terah is none other than the father of Abraham. With Abraham we begin a new story that fills the remaining 39 chapters of Genesis (12-50), a story that details the growing relationship between God and the Patriarchs, and the travels and trials they endure as they wait for the fulfillment of God's promise of progeny and of a homeland. Scholars call these chapters the Epic of the Patriarchs.[37] The term Patriarchs refers to three fathers whom God chose to make into a mighty, numerous people and on whom He would bestow the Promised Land. These are Abraham, his son Isaac, and his son Jacob (also known as Israel).

The term 'epic' is chosen to describe this story because it holds all the characteristics of an epic that could rival Homer's Iliad and Odyssey. It must be long, presenting its esteemed characters in a series of adventures that are held together through their relation to one central figure. The development of episodes within this epic is of utmost importance to the history of the hero's nation. In addition our hero's adventures are presented over a vast setting, with great actions accomplished on their part through valor and courage. At times supernatural forces will intervene. The style of the narrative must be a combination of simplicity and elevated 'poetic' style. Occasionally, too, we will find a narrator contributing side comments about the hero, his deeds or characters he meets.

The Epic of the Patriarch fulfills all these expectations. It is long—thirty-nine chapters. We have our heroes—the Patriarchs. Their adventures are considered a whole because all is accomplished in relation to the central figure, God. The setting is vast. Their movements traverse the Fertile Crescent, a narrow fertile semi-circle of land that stretches from the Persian Gulf northwest through the great river valleys of Mesopotamia (where we find the Tigris and Euphrates rivers), west through northern Syria, following the coast of the Mediterranean through northern Sinai and eventually ending up in the rich river valley of the Nile in Egypt. Mountains flank the upper curve of the Fertile Crescent: the Zagros, the Ararat and Taurus Mountains. Deserts of modern Saudi Arabia and the Sinai stretch below this crescent. Thus the Fertile Crescent was isolated by these two major topographic features and became the geographic playground of the Patriarchs, over which they traveled, living a semi-nomadic lifestyle.

We witness deeds of great valor: Abraham battles the kings of the Canaanite plains, he fights King Abimelech of Gerar's men over water rights; Jacob fights with an 'angel' of God from sunset to sunrise; Joseph is sold into slavery by his brothers, but ends up second to the Pharaoh of Egypt. There are also personal challenges: Abraham is asked to sacrifice his son Isaac; brothers, Jacob and Esau, struggle with each other for power; barren matriarchs endure the sadness of childlessness, then the joy of childbirth. There are humorous episodes (Sarah eavesdropping on Abraham and his divine visitors); episodes of deception (Laban exchanging Rachel for Leah in marriage); and heart wrenching episodes (the death of Rachel in childbirth). The presence of God holds these episodes together, with His divine intervention, His wish to make Abraham and his ancestors His people and He, their God. The literary style is highly readable, though often simplistic in its narrative form. The familiar "and such and such happened, and such and such happened" is interwoven with poetic outbursts and an occasional comment by a narrator. Together all these features create an Epic of Epics.

We might even consider the Epic of the Patriarchs more properly *Epics* of the Patriarchs because we find four cycles emerging in these chapters: the Abraham cycle (Gen. 12-25), the Isaac cycle (Gen. 21-27), the Jacob cycle (Gen. 25-50) and within the Jacob cycle, a Joseph cycle (Gen. 37-50, excluding 38). Cycles overlap with the birth and death of each Patriarch.

As we progress through each cycle we find stories that are comfortingly familiar, others less familiar but essential to carry the plot forward. There are stories that shock our sensibilities; making us question what purpose do they hold? How can they even be included in the Bible? As our cycles unwind we become acquainted with not only the Patriarchs but also the Matriarchs: Sarah, Rebecca, Rachel and Leah. Of these men and women clearly Abraham and his wife Sarah are most crucial to this epic because the promise begins with them and will forever be connected to them. As for Abraham his name and most of his adventures are well known; about Sarah remembrances are mixed. Her world is intertwined with that of Abraham, when she takes center stage her strength eclipses that of Abraham. Just as compelling, too, is the absence of Sarah in some of the most powerful episodes. The journey and adventures of Sarah and Abraham span sixty-two years at which point Sarah dies and Abraham continues another thirty-eight years. To learn about Sarah, then, demands that we retrace the episodes presented in their joint world, acknowledging, however, that while one may be literarily absent he or she is still part of the scene.

From Ur to Canaan

> "These are the descendants of Terah. Terah begat Abram, Nahor and Haran; and Haran begat Lot. And Haran died before his father Terah in the land of his birth, in Ur of the Chaldees. And Abram

and Nahor took for themselves wives; the name of Abram's wife was Sarai, and the name of Nahor's wife was Milcah....Now Sarai was barren; she had no child. Terah took his son Abram and his grandson Lot, son of Haran, and his daughter-in-law Sarai, wife of his son Abram, and they went together from Ur of the Chaldees to go into the land of Canaan; but when they came to Haran, they settled there. The days of Terah were two hundred five years; and Terah died in Haran." (Gen. 11:27-32)

So begins the Epic of the Patriarchs in a coda ('preview') at the end of the genealogy in Genesis 11. Terah, of the lineage of Shem, the favored son of Noah, was the father of Abram. He migrated from his birthplace in Ur of the Chaldees, in Southern Mesopotamia, to Haran in northern Syria, with Abram, his grandson Lot and his daughter-in-law Sarai, Abram's wife. Why he migrated we are not told, though Rabbinic legend[38] relates that it was at Abram's urging. In their home in Ur, where religion was polytheistic, Abram and Sarai's belief in One God and their proselytizing activities had endangered the family. Terah intended to migrate all the way to Canaan, the Promised Land (Gen. 11:31), but traveled only as far as Haran where he eventually died. It was Abram who received the call to move forward to the land of Canaan, taking Sarai and nephew Lot with him (Gen. 12).

The journey of Abraham and Sarah can be divided into early, middle and latter years; a division—as we will see—based on age, but also on their changing personalities. Their names, too, will change in their middle years from Abram and Sarai to Abraham and Sarah. The addition of (or adjustment to) the letter 'h' (Heh in Hebrew) represents the Hebrew word *hamon* 'multitude,' for both Abraham and Sarah become parents of offspring whose progeny will be a 'multitude' of nations (Gen. 17).[39] Their complete journey is chronicled in Gen. 11:27 to Gen. 25:11; from Ur of the Chaldees to Haran, on to Canaan, down to Egypt and back again to Canaan they will travel. Lest the reader think this is a journey of but a few years at most, be forewarned! The episodes may follow one after another, but many years pass between them.

Abraham and Sarah's journey begins from Haran at ages 75 (Gen. 12:4) and 65 respectively (remember Sarah is ten years younger than Abraham is). At what age they migrated from Ur with Terah we are not told, only that they were married.

Sarah's journey will extend from age 65 to 127 when she dies and is buried in the family cave of Machpeleh (Gen. 23:1). Abraham is 137 at her death; he outlives Sarah by 38 years, living to the age of 175 (Gen. 25:7). He will even remarry and bear six more sons! (Gen. 25:1-4). But for 62 years Abraham and Sarah together share a semi-nomadic life, moving in accordance with the will of God.

Who is this Abram whom God choose at age 75 to "go from your country and your kindred and your father's house to the land I will show you" (Gen. 12:1); who received a twofold promise: numerous progeny and land (Gen. 12:1-3) and a promise that most scholars overlook: "I will bless you and make your name great, so that it will be a blessing" (Gen. 12:3)? He is called 'a friend of God' (II Chron. 20:7), a paragon of a faith because of his steadfast belief in God (Gen. 15:6). Who is this Sarai, age 65, who blindly follows her husband to the land God will show him? We know she is barren (Gen. 11:3)—certainly an obstacle to God's promise of progeny, and beautiful (Gen. 12:11). On her death at age 127, legend relates that at one hundred she was as beautiful as when she was twenty, and at twenty she was a virtuous and pure as when she was seven.[40] Tradition dictated that Sarai was "one of 22 women considered 'a woman of valor.'"[41]

These are the images many carry of Abraham and his wife Sarah and there are great truths to these perceptions. But there is more to their portrait; they are indeed virtuous, but they are not perfect. Each and every episode of their cycle contributes one color to their portrait, even when one is absent or in the shadows, an additional daub of paint is applied. Their portrait will change or, better, become more defined as we move through their early to middle to latter years.

The early years of their story begin in Gen. 12, with the focus on Abram; Sarai is a silent Matriarch. In Gen. 12:1-3 the Lord directs Abram:

> "Go from your land and your birthplace and your father's house to the land that I will show you. I will make of you a great nation, and I will bless you, and make your name great, so that it will be a blessing. I will bless those who bless you, and those who curse you I will curse; and in you all the families of the earth shall be blessed."

Abram is promised land, progeny and an esteemed name. Obediently he follows without questioning, taking Sarai and nephew Lot and the rest of his possessions, both material and servants. He is 75; Sarai is 65.

On arriving in Canaan the Lord appears to Abram and again delivers his promises of land and progeny (12:7). We must remember the obstacle, Sarai is barren, but Abram does not question God's words. In Gen. 13, Abram and nephew Lot separate because their flocks and herds were too large for the land to support as one. The Lord again appears to Abram and once again in a dramatic scene using a classic biblical simile, delivers the promises of progeny and land:

> "Raise your eyes now, and look from the place where you are, northward and southward and eastward and westward; for all the land that you see I will give to you and to your offspring forever. I will make your offspring like the dust of the earth; so that if one can count the dust of the earth, your offspring also can be counted. Rise up, walk through the length and the breadth of the land, for I will give it to you" (Gen. 13:14-17).

Abram again does not question God, despite Sarai's barrenness.

> Not until Gen. 15 will Abram speak up and question this childlessness: "O Lord, God, what will you give me, for I continue childless, and the heir of my house is Eliezer of Damascus?...You have

given me no offspring, and so a slave born in my house is to be my heir."

Abram refers to the custom in the Ancient Near East, and documented from such epigraphic evidence as the Nuzi tablets, of childless couples adopting an heir.[42] The Lord's response comes to Abram in a vision in his tent. He bears no anger or impatience at Abram's question, rather he responds to Abram with sincerity, a touchingly human action, and another majestic biblical metaphor. Gently the Lord reassures: "This man [Eliezer] shall not inherit you; rather the one who comes forth from your loins shall inherit you" (Gen. 15:4). And then God escorts Abram outside his tent and directs him to look toward the heavens. As readers we can almost envision God's arm around the shoulders of Abram. Leading him out of the tent, with one arm still around Abram, He extends the other towards heaven and firmly resounds: "Look toward heaven and count the stars, if you are able to count them…thus shall be your seed" (Gen. 15:5)—Abram's progeny will be as numerous as the stars of the heavens. Abram's response is simply belief: "and he believed the Lord; and the Lord reckoned it to him as righteousness" (Gen. 15:6).

God's promise to Abram is sealed by a covenant. In an eerie story found in the remainder of Gen. 15, a heifer, a female goat, a ram are cut in two, with a turtledove and a young pigeon also placed opposite each other. As darkness falls "a smoking fire pot and flaming torch passed between these" making a covenant (literally in Hebrew 'cutting' a covenant) with Abram and his descendants to accept God's promise of land (Gen. 15:18-21).

Abram has been obedient, dutiful and holds a deep respect for and faith in God and His promises; Sarai is the dutiful, silent matriarch. They have lived up to the portrait so many carry in their minds of Abram and Sarai. But before we can go forward toward the fulfillment of these promises, we must backtrack to two important episodes that might temper our impressions of Abram and Sarai. These are the stories in which Sarai will present herself as Abram's sister to protect him, and the story of Abram, mighty man of war.

Sarah, Abraham's Sister? Abraham, Mighty Warrior?

Gen. 12:10—13:1 presents us with a story that has been labeled a 'she is my sister' episode. Abram travels down to Egypt because there was a famine in the land of Canaan. He makes a request of Sarai, "I know that you are a woman beautiful in appearance; and when the Egyptians see you, they will say, 'This is his wife'; then they will kill me, but they will let you live. Say you are my sister, so that it may go well with me because of you, and that my life may be spared on your account" (Gen. 12:11-13). She responds accordingly and is taken to Pharaoh, but God intervenes to protect Sarai. When Pharaoh discovers she is wife not sister to Abram, he releases her and Abram, sending them on their way, as the text suggests, with presents: "now Abram was very rich in livestock, in silver and in gold" (Gen. 13:2).

Technically Abram was not lying, for in Gen. 20:12 we learn that Sarah was indeed Abraham's half-sister: "Besides, she is indeed my sister, the daughter of my father but not the daughter of my mother; and she became my wife." This statement was made in another 'she is my sister' episode, only the venue has changed. This time they are in Gerar, a city near the south in the Negeb.[43] Does this filial relationship lessen the deception perpetrated by Abram? Rabbinic tradition certainly does not find it sufficient.

Rabbinic tradition and the Dead Sea Scrolls emphasize the beauty of Sarah in an attempt to soften the questionable actions of a husband who would put his wife at risk to save his own life. One legend relates[44] how 'chaste' Abraham was, having never before looked at her. On their journey to Egypt from Canaan, as they were crossing a stream, he saw her reflection in the water and saw how exquisitely beautiful she was. Knowing that the Egyptians had a passion for beautiful women, he first tried to hide her in a large produce basket when they entered Egypt. Abraham, however, was too eager to pay the taxes on the produce he brought in, whereby the Egyptians became suspicious, looked in the baskets and seeing how beautiful Sarah was, seized her. All the soldiers became enamored with Sarah, and news of her beauty reached Pharaoh, who had her brought to him. She stated that Abraham was her brother, not the reverse. Sarah willingly chose to protect Abraham.

In the Dead Sea Scrolls, in a text known as the Genesis Apocryphon[45] ('hidden' stories from Genesis), the beauty of Sarah is likewise related.

> "How beautiful is her face? How...fine are the hairs of her head! How lovely are her eyes! How desirable her nose and all the radiance of her countenance...No virgin or bride led into the marriage chamber is more beautiful than she; she is fairer than all other women. Truly, her beauty is greater than theirs. Yet together with all this grace she possesses abundant wisdom, so that whatever she does is perfect!"

In this same text, we also learn of a dream Abraham had the night before his entry into Egypt:

> "and on the night of our entry into Egypt, I, Abram, dreamt a dream; [and behold], I saw in my dream a cedar tree and a palm tree...men came and they sought to cut down the cedar tree and to pull up its roots, leaving the palm tree (standing) alone. But the palm tree cried out saying, 'Do not cut down this cedar tree, for cursed be he who shall fell [it].' And the cedar tree was spared because of the palm tree and [was] not felled."

Sarah is the beautiful palm tree; Abraham is the strong cedar. Rabbinic tradition excuses Abram because the dangerous situation was caused by Sarai's beauty and the result of a dream (perhaps from God) forewarning Abram. Sarai takes the initiative to deceive and thus Abram's character is untarnished. This is legend, not the text.

Can we justify Abram's actions, a man willing to give up his wife to save himself? Perhaps as the chosen progenitor of God's people, his life had to be safeguarded at all costs. Clearly God had a special bond with Abram, a bond only replicated perhaps in his love for King David. We might say that Abram had faith in God; he knew God would protect Sarai. We might also counter that Abram could have placed his faith in God, walking openly with Sarai, his wife, because he trusted that God would protect them in these episodes of their journey, a journey which God had called him to and with whom he had together joined in covenant.

As a sojourner in a foreign land (Egypt) and city-state (Gerar), however, Abram may have been at their mercy, believing his deception was the wisest counterattack. Even with this faith in God, he may have believed he had to work within the laws of the Ancient World, a polytheistic world, and God would determine the outcomes. But Abram's actions become more questionable when we consider the character of Abram in the second of our two overlooked stories.

In Gen. 14 we find the story of Abram and the battle with theKings of the Canaanite plains and the Kings of the East. It follows the Lord's request to Abram to behold all the land he would inherit (Gen. 13). The text relates that three kings from the East had been waging war and subjugating the kingdom of three kings of the Canaanite plains. For twelve years this continued, in the thirteenth year they rebelled, in the fourteenth year the Kings of the East came to fight those in the Plains in the Valley of Siddim (Dead Sea region), plundering regions enroute. Though Abram was only a sojourner in this land, the situation was of great concern because when his nephew Lot had separated from him, Lot had settled in this region, in Sodom. When the kings attacked Sodom, Lot and is family were taken prisoner—the battle was now quite personal for Abram.

The text relates that Abram was living in Hebron, slightly north of the battle, when his allies reported the capture of Lot. We see Abram, the general, the warrior rise to the occasion:

> "When Abram heard that his nephew had been taken captive, he led forth his trained men, born in his house, three hundred eighteen of them, and went in pursuit as far as Dan [northernmost city of Israel]. He divided his forces against them by night, he and his servants, and smote them and pursued them to Hobah, north of Damascus. Then he brought back all the goods, and also brought back his nephew Lot with his goods, and the women and the people" (Gen. 14:14-16).

Abram was a force to be reckoned with, he was strategically minded enough to use the cover of night to ensure his defeat of these kings and rescue Lot and the other inhabitants of Sodom. On his return to the area of (later) Jerusalem, he made a tithe offering to a mysterious King Melchizedek of Salem. The grateful king of Sodom made a request of Abram: "Give me the persons, but take the goods yourself" (Gen. 14:21)—he only wanted the return of his people. Abram returned the inhabitants but declined the offer of the spoils of war, his reasoning "so that you might not say, 'I have made Abram rich'" (Gen. 14:21).

The Abram of Gen. 14 is clearly distinct from the Abram of the 'she is my sister' episodes. Where was his bravery when he and Sarah were endangered? Where were his forces, "his trained men, 318 of them" (Gen. 14:14)? We might argue that 318 men would be insignificant against the Egyptian forces or to those of the King of Gerar. This may indeed be true! But where is this brave Abram and why was he so hesitant to accept the spoils of war, but not the spoils of deception as he left Egypt (Gen. 13:1) and later Gerar (Gen. 20:14).

This story and the 'she is my sister' episodes add an oft-overlooked dimension to the portrait of Abram and Sarai. We know Abram is righteous and a man of faith. We can now add a mighty man of war, a man who without hesitation went to the aid of his nephew Lot. Certainly these are attributes of a hero, an esteemed man. Given his bravery on the battlefield, his actions in relation to his wife Sarai are even more difficult to defend. Where is the bravery, his faith in God or his love 'without bounds' for Sarai. Do we dismiss Abram's actions, as feminists suggest, as an example of the misogynist treatment of women in the Bible?

What about Sarai? Do these episodes alter our initial impression of her as the dutiful, obedient and silent matriarch? Hardly! If anything the 'she is my sister' episodes reveal her to be either obedient or submissive (and we will have to reconsider the second 'she is my sister' episode in the setting of her middle years). It may indeed be submission out of love or lack of a viable option. Could Sarai have said, 'No! I will not misrepresent myself?' Given the nature of the Ancient World this seems improbable. When Abram battles the Kings of the Canaanite plains we can assume Sarai stayed back at their tent in Hebron, the dutiful wife, the silent wife. Throughout the early years of their journey Sarai has remained dutiful and uniformly silent. She is spoken to, but she herself has never uttered a word; the narrator related her actions. Will Sarai remain the dutiful, silent matriarch? Will she ever gain her voice? As we move into the middle years of their journey such will not be the case! Sarai will gain her voice, but at what expense to Abram? The actions and words of both in their middle years will cause us to again rethink our impressions of the characters of Abram and Sarai as we continue to develop their portrait.

Sarah Finds Her Voice

As Gen. 16 opens the setting is still Canaan, the time ten years later (16:3); Abram is now 85, Sarai 75. We are reminded, "Now Sarai, Abram's wife, bore him no children." Following this information, Sarai will find her voice! Since God did not grant her or prevented her from having a child, she found another way of obtaining a child. She took matters into her own hands and in keeping with ancient customs, gave her Egyptian slave-girl Hagar to Abram. And then we hear the *first words* of Sarai. They are spoken to Abram, "You see that the Lord has prevented me from bearing children; go in to my slave-girl; it may be that I shall obtain children by her" (Gen. 16:2). Abram's response is simply, "and Abram listened to the voice of Sarai" (Gen. 16:2). In keeping with the custom of the day, Abram is not required to be monogamous, but what is unique is that it is Sarai who suggests that he take another wife. Hagar is not just a concubine for the text says "Sarai, Abram's wife, took Hagar the Egyptian, her slave-girl, and gave her to her husband as a wife" (Gen. 16:3).

As our story progresses we will have mixed emotions about Sarai, Hagar and Abram. At age 75, Abram "went in to Hagar and she conceived" (Gen. 16:4). Though Sarai wished for Abram to have a child, as readers we can't help but wonder how Sarai felt learning her handmaid had conceived so quickly in Abram's embrace. Hagar's response to her conception is troublesome; she holds contempt for Sarai. Literally the Hebrew text means that her mistress was esteemed little in her eyes. Sarai then looked to Abram to resolve this issue: "May the wrong done to me be on you! I gave my slave-girl to your embrace, and when she saw that she had conceived, she looked on me with contempt. May the Lord judge between you and me" (Gen. 16:5). The mighty Abram responds "your slave-girl is in your power; do to her as you please" (Gen. 16:6). Abram stands in the middle of these two women, but the decision goes to Sarai, for as mistress of the house, Hagar is still subject to her authority. Sarai's response, "Then Sarai dealt harshly with her, and she ran away from her" (Gen. 16:6). Our silent, dutiful matriarch now shows different attributes.

The biblical text may be silent about the manner of Hagar's contempt or the form of Sarai's harshness, but Rabbinic literature addresses both these issues. Sarai believed that her barrenness was due to her own fault, thus without any jealousy she gave her slave Hagar to Abram, instructing her first in their beliefs and making of her a freed woman so she could be worthy of Abram. As soon as Hagar learned she was with child, Hagar began to treat Sarai with contempt by disparaging Sarai to the other women of the camp. Hagar claimed that Sarai was barren because she was not as righteous and pious as she presented herself. Hagar, thus, hoped to assume Sarai's position in the household. [46] Abram was ready to defend Sarai, giving her full power to deal with Hagar; however, he reminded her that since Hagar was freed, Sarai could not return her to an enslaved state. This is where Sarai's harshness enters the picture. Sarai made her serve as a slave by tending to Sarai's ablutions. This is what forced Hagar to flee to the wilderness.[47] Though Rabbinic legend may provide us with the answers to Hagar's contempt and Sarai's harshness, they are legends devised to explain troubling passages. The biblical text remains silent; however, our sympathies are torn from one woman to the other, and Abram, at this point, does not interfere with the workings of his household; this is the matriarch's domain.

Fleeing to the wilderness, Hagar is met by an angel of the Lord and told to submit to her mistress. Our sympathies are again pulled toward Hagar. The figure of Hagar deserves special attention in her own right, but what is so very unique is while in the wilderness she is the first of either gender to receive an annunciation in the biblical text. She is told that her child will be named Ishmael "God hears" and her offspring will be innumerable. She, a woman, is the first to give the Lord a name, El-roi "God (who) sees." The story concludes, "Hagar bore Abram a son; and Abram named his son, whom Hagar bore, Ishmael. Abram was eighty-six years old when Hagar bore him Ishmael" (Gen. 16:15-16). Abram gives the child the name decreed by the angel. Abram is now 86, Sarai 76. One year has passed from the beginning to end of Chapter 16. One year that dramatically changed the life of Sarai, Abram and Hagar.

For the next thirteen years the text will be silent. Our journey continues in Gen. 17:1 "when Abram was ninety-nine years old." What happens in these 13 years we are not told, even Rabbinic literature glosses over the gap in time. Did the Lord speak to Abram? Continue to give encouragement and blessings? Did Abram and Sarai assume Ishmael was the fulfillment of God's promise of progeny? For 13 years we do not know what transpired between God and Abram and Sarai and Hagar. Perhaps we must just imagine that they continued in their gradual movements from place to place, tending to their herds, together watching with joy as the baby Ishmael grew to the significant age of 13.

In Gen. 17 we are told that Abram was 99, (thus Sarai was 89). Abram's name is changed, "No longer shall your name be Abram, but your name shall be Abraham, for I have made you the ancestor of a multitude of nations" (Gen. 17:5). Sarai's name, too, is changed, "As for Sarai your wife, you shall not call her Sarai, but Sarah shall be her name" (Gen. 17:15). The addition of the letter /h/ in Abram's name and the alteration of the /i/ of Sarai to Sarah represents the Hebrew word *hamon* "multitude." From both Abraham and Sarah a multitude of nations would arise. This name change is a harbinger of good fortune. Abraham's reaction is laughter "Can a child be born to a man who is a hundred years old? Can Sarah, who is ninety years old, bear a child?" (Gen. 17:17). His laughter foreshadows the son who will be born to them, Isaac, meaning "one who laughs"; Isaac will bring the fulfillment of promises, not Ishmael. Gen. 17 closes with the sign of the covenant—the circumcision of Abraham, Ishmael and all the men of his household.

With Gen. 18 we are provided a unique glimpse of the workings and customs of a semi-nomadic household. Abraham is seated at the entrance to his tent in the heat of the day. Three 'men' approach and he responds with hospitality. The offer of hospitality and acceptance were paramount among the laws of the ancient world. A host would protect his guests above all else; to decline an offer of hospitality would be a great insult. Thus, Abraham sends Sarah to prepare refreshments for their visitors, giving us a glimpse of her domain. While Sarah is off in preparation, one of the messengers delivers an annunciation to Abraham, "I will surely return to you in due season, and your wife Sarah shall have a son" (Gen. 18:10). Sarah, eavesdropping, was astonished. They were both advanced in age and "it had ceased to be with Sarah after the manner of women" (Gen. 18:11). Her response, "she laughed to herself" (Gen. 18:12). The Lord questioned why she laughed, but when quizzed by Abraham she denied it. This entire discourse is built on the interplay of the Hebrew root /ts-h-q/ meaning "to laugh" and foreshadows the birth of the one who brought laughter as a gift from God, none other than Abraham and Sarah's son Isaac (Gen. 21:6).

In Gen. 21, Sarah does indeed conceive and bear a son for Abraham in his old age. Abraham names the child Isaac as foretold; he is circumcised according to the covenant at eight days old (Gen. 17:10-12). Abraham is 100 and Sarah is 90. Sarah's joy resounds in her words, "God has brought laughter for me; everyone who hears will laugh with me...Who would have ever said to Abraham that Sarah would nurse children? Yet I have borne him a son in his old age" (Gen. 21:6-7).

A few years pass and Isaac is weaned; Abraham throws a great feast in his honor and Sarah, who so joyously reveled in the laughter that God gave her and Abraham, turns harsh once again. "But Sarah saw the son of Hagar the Egyptian, whom she had borne to Abraham, playing with her son Isaac" (Gen. 21:9). The key to Sarah's actions involves the meaning of the word "playing." It is derived from the same three letters as Isaac's name /ts-h-q/. But it is a verbal form in a conjugation that indicates intensity. Rabbinic tradition[48] relates that this verb has sexual connotations, as in Gen. 26:10 where Isaac is seen "fondling" his wife Rebecca. Ishmael, legend relates, was doing something immoral with Isaac that repulsed Sarah. Sarah does not ask Abraham for help, rather she tells him "cast out this slave woman with her son; for the son of this slave woman shall not inherit along with my son Isaac" (Gen. 21:10). Abraham is distressed, but God directs him to follow Sarah's order, "for it is through Isaac that offspring shall be named for you" (Gen. 21:12). However, God also assures Abraham that his other son Ishmael will also be a mighty nation, because he is Abraham's offspring (Gen. 21:13). Hagar is expelled to the wilderness once again. This time she will not return. As hope flees, an angel of God comes to their aid and they thrive. Ishmael eventually takes a wife from his mother's homeland of Egypt, to return only for the burial of his father Abraham (Gen. 25:9).

Abraham and Sarah now have the promised son, Isaac, he who brings laughter to all and with whom are the future promises. The middle years of Abraham and Sarah have been tumultuous. Sarah's personality seems to have changed. In the confines of her home she is bold, harsh, in control. She forced Hagar to flee when her position as matriarch was threatened. She demanded that Hagar and Ishmael be cast out when in some way her son, Isaac, was threatened. Our silent matriarch has found her voice! But are we happy with its resonance. Where her position or her son is endangered, Sarah becomes the Matriarch in control. We cannot help but rejoice when Sarah's burden of barrenness is lifted, but we cannot help but temper our joy when we witness her harsh side. Do we excuse or attribute Sarah's boldness to her threatened position or more importantly to her motherly instincts to protect her son Isaac at all costs? Do we accept the friction between Sarah and Hagar as a story serving to explain the friction that exists until this day between Jews and Muslims? Should we say it is all part of God's plan? Our portrait of Sarah as the dutiful, obedient, submissive wife must be revised.

As for Abram turned Abraham, the familiar portrait of the dutiful, obedient, mighty warrior, faithful man of God has already been tempered in the early years with his cowardly (?) behavior on entry into Egypt. His middle years still display a strong respect for God, but with matters of the hearth, Abraham gives way to Sarah (16:6), then the Lord's wishes (Gen. 21:11-12). As we finish the middle and latter years of the journey, new traits will be added to his character, traits that may not be too pleasing. Just as their early years contained disturbing stories, so too do their middle into latter years.

Abraham's Mistakes?

Would that I could end the journey of Abraham and Sarah in their middle years. Abraham's portrait has already been questioned by his cowardice (?) in not defending his wife and by his deference to Sarah in the treatment of Hagar. These stories were sufficient to teach us that

Abraham is not perfect. As for Sarah, though her early years saw her as a dutiful, silent matriarch, her voice resounded loud and clear in her middle years. She was in charge where matters of the hearth and of her son, Isaac, were concerned. She, too, is not perfect. But within their middle years I must return to two troubling episodes.

One story is that of Abraham's plea for the righteous of the city of Sodom (Gen. 18) and how it directly bears on his character in perhaps the most crucial story in the Abraham cycle, the Sacrifice (more properly the Binding) of Isaac (Gen. 22). The other story is another 'she is my sister episode' in Gen. 20—recall in their early years a similar situation prevailed (Gen. 12).

Abraham has already been duly chastised for his actions in Gen. 12 where he asked Sarai to pose as his sister to save himself from the Egyptians. But this same situation occurs once again in Gen. 20. This time the deception is perpetrated on Abimelech, King of Gerar. This time God himself intervenes in a dream: "Yes, I know that you [Abimelech] did this in the integrity of your heart; furthermore it was I [God] who kept you from sinning against me" (Gen. 20:6). Abraham is called to account for his deception before Abimelech: "And Abimelech said to Abraham, 'What were you thinking of, that you did this thing?' Abraham said, 'I did it because I thought, There is no fear of God at all in this place, and they will kill me because of my wife" (Gen. 20:10-11). Where is Abraham's faith in his God? Did he not yet understand that his God, unlike those of Canaan, Egypt and Mesopotamia, transcended time and space? Moreover Abraham tries to excuse himself by revealing that Sarah is in fact his half-sister; they share the same father. He had already planned this manner of deception before he left Haran: "And when God caused me to wander from my father's house, I said to her, 'This is the kindness you must do me: at every place to which we come, say of me, He is my brother'." (Gen. 20:13) The text does not say Sarah had agreed; but perhaps her actions indicate she did acquiesce. Abraham received gifts of livestock and servants from Abimelech; Sarah receives one thousand pieces of silver as a symbol of her exoneration. And then something unique happens. Abraham prays on behalf of Abimelech, for when Sarah was taken all the women and female servants "wombs had closed fast" (Gen. 20:18). They were now open, free to conceive and bear children.

In this detail we find an important literary link to the next story. In Gen. 21:1-2 we learn, "The Lord dealt with Sarah as he had said, and the Lord did for Sarah as he promised. Sarah conceived and bore Abraham a son in his old age, at the time of which God had spoken to him." Sarah, once barren, was no longer so. She gave birth to Isaac. A literary critic would say this 'she is my sister' episode introduces and serves to emphasize the miraculous fulfillment of God's promise that Sarah would have a son. This literary connection might explain the purpose of this story and we might say Abraham did it once so certainly it must be common place or at least an understandable situation; however, the circumstances are quite different here than in their early years. Abraham has another wife, Hagar, and a son Ishmael—we hear nothing of them. Moreover, both Abraham and Sarah now know that Sarah herself is to bear a child. We even know his name, Isaac. Sarah may even be with child when she feigns the ruse. (Does the conception referred to in Gen. 21:1 happen after Gen. 20 or had she already conceived?) Do we chastise both Abraham for his lack of faith and courage and Sarah for her lack of faith and for jeopardizing the birth of her son for the safety of Abraham? Sarah exhibited such strength when her household position was challenged by Hagar or later when her son was in some way endangered. Why would she endanger her unborn son? Where is her courage and boldness?

Let us turn to our second troublesome story, Abraham's defense of the righteous of Sodom (Gen. 18) and how this relates to one of the most famous stories, the Sacrifice of Isaac. In Gen. 18, the same three 'men' who visited Abraham and Sarah with news of the annunciation of Isaac, also tell of the impending destruction of the wicked city of Sodom.

Abraham guides these three 'men' for a while on their journey and then the Lord comes down to see for himself the wickedness of Sodom and Gomorrah (Gen. 18:21). God revealed to Abraham what he was about to do (Gen. 18:19) and the two 'stood' together as Abraham begins an unrelenting plea for the righteous of Sodom: "Suppose there are fifty righteous within the city; will you then sweep away the place and not forgive it for the fifty righteous who are in it?" (Gen. 21:24) Abraham is bold: "Far be it from you to do such a thing, to slay the righteous with the wicked, so that the righteous fare as the wicked! Far be that from you! Shall the Judge of all the earth do what is just?" (Gen. 18:25). The Lord acquiesces to fifty. Remember Abraham's nephew Lot and family live in Sodom and Abraham knew of their nature; he had rescued them from the Kings of the East in Gen. 14. Fearful for his nephew and that there might not be fifty righteous there, Abraham, the bargainer, jumps into action. If not 50, how about 45, 40, 30, 20 and then just 10. The bargaining stops; both the Lord and Abraham go their ways. Apparently there were not even ten righteous in Sodom, for Sodom is destroyed, but 'two' messengers do warn Lot (Gen. 19).

This story presents a side of Abraham we have never seen. Indeed he may be respectful of the Lord: "Oh do not let the Lord be angry if I speak just once more" (Gen. 18:32), but he is bold and persistent. Where is the Abraham who did not question God's promise of progeny until Gen. 15? Who laughed first when he was told Sarah was to have a child? More importantly where is *this* Abraham when in Gen. 22 God tests Abraham saying, "Take your son, your only son Isaac, whom you love, and go to the land of Moriah, and offer him there as a burnt offering on one of the mountains that I will show you" (Gen. 22:2)? Where, too, is Sarah, Isaac's mother? Isaac is in fact Sarah's only son, not Abraham's. Where is the protective mother when God asks Abraham to sacrifice her only son? Would she have known how Abraham had pleaded for the righteous of Sodom and wondered why he would not plead for the life of his son and her only son? Our examination of the Sacrifice of Isaac will take us into the latter years of Abraham and Sarah. This story is the apex of their journey for afterwards they will but briefly be mentioned.

The Sacrifice of Isaac

> "He [God] said to him, "Abraham!" And he said, "Here I am." He said, "Take your son, your only son Isaac, whom you love, go to the land of Moriah, and offer him there as a burnt offering on one of the mountains that I shall show you." (Gen. 22:1b-2)

These words are preceded by the statement: "After these things God tested Abraham" (Gen. 22:1a). After what things! After a life already filled with trials and tribulations, with happiness and sadness, with faith and with questions. Now comes the final test, the climax in the final years of his physical and spiritual journey.

Tradition has seen in this story, the Aqedah (Sacrifice, literally, the Binding of Isaac), the keystone of the arch of Abraham's life as the paragon of faith. When God called to him, he responded with the Hebrew phrase of immediacy and acquiescence: *hinneni* "Here I am!" When told to take his son and offer him on the mountain God would show him, Abraham dutifully followed orders: "So Abraham rose early in the morning, saddled his donkey, and took two of his young men with him, and his son Isaac; he cut the wood for the burnt offering, and set out and went to the place in the distance that God had shown him" (Gen. 22:3). When he reached the destination he ordered his servants to stay behind with the donkey and then took the wood of the offering and placed it on Isaac's back to carry; Abraham took the fire and knife. The text relates, "So the two of them walked on together" (Gen. 22:6)—a beautiful image of father and son. But what of the destination? Isaac knows something is amiss, for he notes that there is no lamb for the sacrifice. Abraham responds, "God himself will provide the lamb for the burnt offering, my son. (Gen. 22:8)" And again we have that beautifully innocent, touching parent-child scene of Abraham and

Isaac walking on together. "When they came to the place that God had shown him, Abraham built an altar there and laid the wood in order. He bound his son Isaac, and laid him on the altar, on top of the wood" (Gen. 22:9). And Isaac said not a word. "Then Abraham reached out his hand and took the knife to kill his son. But the angel of the Lord called to him from heaven and said, "Abraham, Abraham!" And he said again, *hinneni* "Here I am." He said, "Do not lay your hand on the boy or do anything to him; for now I know that you fear God, since you have not withheld your son, your only son, from me" (Gen. 10-12). Magically a ram appears in the thicket, offered up instead of his son. Did Abraham pass the test? Apparently so for again the angel of the Lord appears to Abraham, reaffirming God's promises of progeny and land.

This story as taught to me and to many others depicted Abraham as the paragon of faith. He didn't question God as to why God would want him to sacrifice his son, who was so long awaited, the son who was to be the fulfillment of God's promise of progeny. The issue was simply that Abraham blindly followed God's orders, trusting in whatever plan God had laid, creating the portrait of the man of perfect faith. Has Abraham returned to the Abram of his early years, the dutiful Abraham who did not question, who blindly followed God? Where is the Abraham who fought the Kings of the East or more importantly the Abraham who bargained with God over the righteous of Sodom? Why did Abraham not speak up on behalf of his son Isaac? He had seen his son Ishmael banished to the wilderness with Hagar, though distressed by the circumstances he agreed because God told him his future was with Isaac. So perhaps Abraham unswervingly followed God's commands in Genesis 22. The strength of Abraham's conviction in God's plan demonstrated his faith in his God.

It is this determination and unswerving faith that Rembrandt captured in his Sacrifice of Isaac. His Abraham may be gray-haired but he is strong; he grasps the face of his son pulling him back *firmly*, exposing Isaac's neck. The knife begins to fall from his other hand because the angel has *firmly* grasped that arm, preventing him from slashing the throat of his son. Abraham has one focus—to sacrifice his son as God commanded; he appears surprised to see the angel. This is the vision of Abraham that has come down through history.

But there are questions in this story: Abraham is asked to sacrifice his son, his only son Isaac—but Isaac is not his only son. There is also Ishmael—Islamic tradition indeed records Ishmael as the son to be sacrificed. Why doesn't Isaac question what his father was about to do? Like Jesus he carries the wood of his sacrifice, walking acceptingly toward his end. Indeed Christianity sees in this story the prefiguration of the crucifixion of Jesus. Rabbinic tradition, too, preserves varied stories of Isaac in this situation. Why does God give the command to sacrifice, but an angel of God deliver the stay and reiterate God's promises? These questions beg thought. The meaning and significance of this story, too, changes depending on the circumstances of one's life. Rembrandt's painting was done when in the prime of his life, at the height of his career with a devoted wife and four loving children. Twenty years later Rembrandt presented another portrait of the Sacrifice of Isaac, better described as a simple pencil sketch. The lines are weak; Abraham is old, frail, with hollowed cheeks and sunken eyes. His arm embraces his son-cradled face downward in his lap; his other arm loosely holds the knife that is almost falling from his grasp. The angel floats almost invisibly in the background, as if little effort is required to stay the command of Abraham. Rembrandt's life had changed, he had lost his beloved wife and four children to disease—how could Rembrandt depict vigor in the sacrifice of another man's child if he himself had lost so much! How could God test in such a way and how could we not understand Abraham as deep in despair?

We must ask, too, where was Sarah? She is not mentioned in the biblical text, she is the absent wife as in the early years? Isaac is her only son, not Abraham's. Isaac is the child who made her so protective of her domain so much so that a harsh unflattering side of her personality emerged. Would she not have spoken up on behalf of her son as Abraham had for the righteous of Sodom?

Rabbinic tradition responds to Sarah's absence in legend. One tradition records that Abraham did tell Sarah, under the guise of deception. Abraham told Sarah that he was taking Isaac to study the Torah with esteemed elders. Though saddened that he would be away for a while, she selected a beautiful garment for him to wear, and 'with great weeping' accompanied them at the beginning of their journey.[49]

Another tradition relates that Satan appeared as an old man and told Sarah the truth: "In this hour Sarah's loins trembled, and all her limbs shook. She was no more of this world."[50] Another version relates that Satan spoke to Sarah; when Abraham returned home alone she realized that Satan spoke the truth. She was "so grieved that her soul fled from her body."[51] Contemporary interpreters have also suggested that the ram magically appearing entangled in the thicket was none other than Sarah. Entangled because she had to be withheld from preventing the sacrifice of her only son or from offering herself in his stead. Marc Chagall's depiction of the Aqedah may suggest as much, for almost imperceptibly hidden in the thicket peers out a ram. Perhaps this story delivers a larger message; that God, unlike the pagan gods of the nations about the Fertile Crescent, did not want human sacrifice. Or is it sufficient to say Isaac was a gift by divine intervention, thus God could take him back whenever he so chose? A contemporary midrash by Betty Lieberman expresses a mother's pain on hearing this passage read each year at the festival of Rosh Hashanah (New Year):

> *I sat there and listened to the Rabbi say this is the ultimate story of love of God, of trust in God, of man's perfect faith in God; and I was uncomfortable as I have been for years. And I wondered what would have happened if God had called on Sarah to bring Isaac to Him instead of Abraham. Would we live in a different world today? Would we place a different value on human life, on our children, on ourselves?*
>
> *Would Sarah have felt differently about sacrificing her child? I ask myself if any woman would have obediently brought her child to God.*

Or would Sarah, who had carried Isaac in her womb for nine months, who had felt the first gentle movements of his body in hers, whose body had nourished him through nine months of pregnancy and whose milk had nourished him as an infant...could Sarah, who nurtured him through his childhood, have offered him to God in perfect faith as Abraham did?

I do not believe she could. Isaac is the issue of Abraham's seed, one of thousands; but he was a part of Sarah, and she a part of him. He would have been too precious to Sarah. And would not Sarah, like any mother, have offered herself in preference to her child. Would she not have bargained with God, as women have bargained through the centuries; he is too precious, too beautiful, his future too important; do not take him, take me!

With no less faith than Abraham had, I believe Sarah would have denied God her child and offered herself instead. And God, seeing the sincerity of her love for Him, would have understood, as he understood Abraham.

And the generations that followed would have understood the story differently. Because as Abraham was able to face the sacrifice of his child, so have generations that followed discounted the value of each individual life. How many human beings have been sacrificed through the centuries in the name of God? How many human beings have we watched being killed as we stood quietly by and professed our faith in a loving and just God?

If Sarah had been tested and told God, "I will not sacrifice my child. He is too precious," would the world be different today? Would she be the role model for every woman who did not want to send her son to war—and so would wars be ended? Would the powerful have the role model (Abraham) to bind up the powerless and trusting (Isaac)? Would women see themselves as full human beings acknowledged and respected by God for their ability to protect themselves and their children instead of as dependents of men? Would the world see children as human beings to be nurtured and protected instead of mentally and physically battered? Would we know that every human being is of equal value because every human being is of woman-born?

Is it too late to rewrite history and the Torah?[52]

We feel a mother's pain in Lieberman's response to the Aqedah, the pain, the courage, the altruism that is surely shared by other women in reaction to this passage. Whether we try to recreate this story through the eyes and heart of a woman, as Lieberman so eloquently does, or whether we look to Rabbinic tradition as a guide, or whether we hold fast to the traditional, sadly the same literary results follow. Abraham and his servants return and settle in Beersheba, a brief genealogy intervenes, and we are presented with the death of Sarah. Is it just coincidental? Sarah abruptly leaves the picture. We then hear the only tender words expressing Abraham's love for Sarah: "and Abraham went to mourn for Sarah and to weep for her" (Gen. 23:2). Abraham purchases the family burial cave at Machpeleh (Gen. 23); Sarah is now referred to as "my dead" (Gen. 23:4) or "his dead" (Gen. 23:3). From a contemporary perspective, an unloving epithet to give the woman with whom you traversed the fertile crescent, with whom you finally shared the joy of a child, and a woman who twice endangered her life to save yours! Sarah's journey is over.

We will hear of Sarah in Gen. 24:36. She is referred to as 'my master's wife who bore a son [Isaac]' by Abraham's servant who was sent to Aram-Naharaim to bring a wife back for Isaac from their next of kin. In Gen. 24:67, Sarah is again referenced, when this wife, Rebekah, is brought back for Isaac: "Then Isaac brought her into his mother Sarah's tent. He took Rebekah, and she became his wife; and he loved her. So Isaac was comforted after his mother's death." Here we sense a son's deep love for his mother, comforted, but not replaced by a wife's love. Lastly, we hear of Sarah in 25:10 when Abraham is laid to rest beside her.

Abraham's story is near its end, but as noted in Gen. 24 Abraham goes at great lengths to procure a wife for his son Isaac. In Gen. 25:1 comes a surprise for many a biblical student: "Abraham took another wife, whose name was Keturah." Who this Keturah is is a mystery. Rabbinic legend says she is none other than Hagar, whom Isaac traveled to the land of Egypt to bring back to comfort his father after the death of Sarah. She bears Abraham six sons—legend relates that from them descended some of the nastiest tribes in the Ancient Near East. Abraham's remarriage and procreation may surprise some, but we must remember that he outlived Sarah by 38 years; Isaac, however, still inherits all (Gen. 25:5).

Abraham's journey comes to an end: "this is the length of Abraham's life, one hundred and seventy-five years. Abraham breathed his last and died in a good old age, an old man and full of years, and was gathered to his people" (Gen. 25:7-8). Both Isaac and Ishmael are present at the internment of their father, as Abraham is laid to rest beside Sarah.

The final years of Abraham and Sarah are dominated by the Aqedah, the Binding of Isaac. All else pales in comparison to this final story. The question is how do we relate this story to our portrait of Abraham and Sarah. Do we view this story as the apex of their faith or the tribulation that brought their journey to its end? Sarah certainly is removed from the picture quickly and although Abraham lives on to take another wife and bear SIX more sons, this information is anticlimactic. The Aqedah is the final defining story of both their characters. Looking only at the biblical text, Sarah is absent, we cannot even say silent with certainty and Abraham is dutiful. Their characters have come full circle; they are back to the attributes of their early years.

Abraham and Sarah, a 'Perfect' Portrait (?)

Beersheba, a city on the fringe of the Negeb. Abraham returned here after the attempted sacrifice of his son Isaac to set up camp for the last time with his wife Sarah. From here their final journey would be northeast to Hebron where Sarah dies and will be buried nearby. Their journey, in keeping with the characteristics of an epic, has reached far and wide, was filled with adventures, with divine intervention, with the miraculous. It is a journey that has revealed the character of Abraham and Sarah; it a journey perhaps that has influenced them as well.

The reader can envision their portrait as created by two strands interwoven—like a tapestry. Of the two strands, one—let's call it the vertical strand reaching from earth to heaven—is the perfect strand. Its threads, colors and hues are those we imagine in fairy tales, and wishful thinking, creating an image we strive for or should strive for—an essential image of goodness, obedience, a respect for duty to someone or something that is bigger than we are. Then there is the human strand—let's call it the horizontal strand extending from the beginning to the end of one's life. This is the strand of personal goals and desires that can get in the way of a larger goal, the rites of passage through which all must pass, filled with incidents that may at times contribute the shadows to our portrait; it is a necessary, but imperfect strand.

The perfect strand of Abraham is found in his early, middle and final years. It is the Abram who left his homeland at God's behest without question, who accepted God's promise of progeny and land despite Sarai's barrenness and his semi-nomadic lifestyle, it is the Abram who believes that Eliezer his adopted heir will not inherit because God says so. It is an Abram who makes a covenant with God agreeing to all that God commands. It is an Abraham who rejoices with laughter at the birth of his second son Isaac. It is an Abraham who accepts his wife's expulsion of his son Ishmael and his 'wife' Hagar because God directs him to. It is the Abraham that without question went up to Moriah to sacrifice his son.

The imperfect strand of Abram surfaces in his role of mighty warrior, saving Lot, his family and the Sodomites; not that bravery is imperfect, but his bravery here makes us question how he could have endangered Sarah in Egypt, passing her off as his wife and again in Gerar, when he knew she was either pregnant with Isaac or about to conceive. It was the imperfect Abraham that acquiesced to Sarah's harsh treatment of Hagar. It was the imperfect strand that displays the bold Abraham who bargains for the righteous of Sodom, but says nothing in defense of his son when asked to sacrifice him.

As for Sarah the perfect strand appears as she dutifully follows Abram/Abraham throughout the Fertile Crescent serving as the silent matriarch, bearing the burden of her barrenness. It is the perfect Sarah that agrees to pass herself off as Abram's sister in Egypt. It is the perfect Sarah who rejoices with laughter at the birth of Isaac. It is the perfect Sarah who does not prevent Abraham in his attempted sacrifice of Isaac.

It is the imperfect Sarai who gives her handmaid Hagar to Abram as a wife in order to force the hand of God into giving Abram a son. It is the imperfect Sarah who laughs at the news of a woman her age conceiving. It is the imperfect Sarah who endangers the child she is to bear, Isaac, by feigning to be Abraham's wife in Gerar. It is the imperfect Sarah who treats Hagar and Ishmael with harshness.

Together these two strands present an imperfect portrait, with each portrait almost a mirror image of the other, distinguished perhaps only by gender. This portrait realistically portrays the nature of humans, making Sarah and Abraham feasible, tangible role models. They are not perfect; they are not meant to be. Does this mean Abraham's actions of cowardice, deception, indifference, lack of boldness or Sarah's harshness, boldness, perhaps outright cruelty, are to be excused. No! It only means that they were flawed, they were human. We can be angry and frustrated and embarrassed by their actions and responses. But in a sense their flaws added to their acts of faithfulness and beliefs are what endears them to us so much more. They never claimed perfection, or perfect faithfulness; history or rather distorted history proclaimed it of them.

"And the generations that followed would have understood the story differently," writes Lieberman of revisiting the Aqedah. Similarly, by revisiting the Epic of Abraham and Sarah, we and the generations to follow can understand this Epic cycle differently, seeing the 'perfect' portrait of Abraham and Sarah as one painted to perfection by acknowledging their imperfections as the imperfections of humanity.

◆　　◆　　◆

Her name is Sara, without the 'h'—mom chose the name, dad the spelling, as she is wont to note. To mom the choice of name reflected a passion for the biblical narrative, the strength of a biblical matriarch, a harbinger of a strong woman, a name befitting a child and a woman. Dad perceived the name as feminine, yet commanding of respect when she entered the world of business, medicine or law. As the years passed and this Sara, our Sara, entered her early teens, having revisited the biblical legacy of Sarah and Abraham, I questioned bestowing this name on our first-born. Perhaps I should have studied the biblical text a bit more carefully fourteen years ago! Through my writings and lectures my husband, too, has become acquainted with the biblical Sarah; however, he is not concerned with our name choice. He is more pleased with our Sara's success in school, her musical ability, her gift of conversation and, of course, socializing, but even more so he is relieved that her aspirations to become a corn vendor was but the phase of a four year old living in the farm country of Wisconsin!

Grateful though I am that her career potentials have moved beyond the corn vendor phase, my thoughts still turn to the character of Sara's namesake. Would she become the submissive, obedient Sarah, the harsh Sarah, the rejoicing Sarah? In my Sara I certainly see rejoicing, but submissiveness—undeniably no, and obedience—a matter of degree. As for harshness, this attribute has fortunately not surfaced, save during 'healthy' sibling squabbles. During these squabbles I have not been remiss to remind her that someday younger brother Alexander may rise up like Alexander the Great or Czar Alexandre (the namesake of his native country) and take dominion! Like the biblical Sarah, my Sara laughs in disbelief.

Sodom and Beyond: Lot and His Daughters

Mention the cities of Sodom and Gomorrah and most people will equate these cities with the ultimate in wickedness, drinking without restraint, debauchery, illicit sex and, in particular, sodomy. These cities were so evil that not even ten righteous could be found in them so that God would spare them (Gen. 18). Within this city, Lot, Abraham's nephew, was living. As the city was about to be destroyed two angels warned Lot, so that Lot, his wife and two daughters were able to flee as fire and brimstone rained down upon the wicked cities, forever destroying them from the face of the earth. So familiar, too, is what we believe is the ending of this story: "Lot's wife, behind him, looked back and she became a pillar of salt" (Gen. 19:26). Not only is there a missing detail or two to this story, but the story extends beyond that eternal image of Lot's wife frozen into a pillar of salt, looking back toward Sodom and Gomorrah, a pillar equated by many with the salt configurations that skirt the desolate waters of the Dead Sea.

A closer reading of Genesis 19 reveals the story does not simply recall the destruction of these two cities. The focus is on Sodom, Lot's home, AND there is a story before its destruction and after it. The story begins—two angels come to Sodom at evening, meeting Lot, Abraham's nephew at the gates of the city. Lot greeted them and offered them hospitality—lodging for the night, washing of their feet after a long, dusty journey. Initially they turn down his offer, but Lot insists. They return home with him; a feast is prepared. But before they are able to turn in for the night, unexpected guests come to call—the men of Sodom, young and old, every one, the text records (Gen. 19:4). They surround the house and call out to Lot:

> *Where are the men who came to you tonight? Bring them out to us, so that we may know them.* (Gen. 19:5)

'Know' in the biblical sense means to have sexual relations. Here the intimation is clear and even more horrendous. Envision the situation—perhaps you may not wish to—all the men of Sodom, from the youngest to oldest (an expression meaning 'all encompassing') desire to have sexual relations with these two divine visitors. One might argue they did not know these were 'undercover angels,' but this is irrelevant. Whether the men are divine or human the action implied is repulsive.

The story continues. Lot goes out to try to appease them. He has offered these two men/angels hospitality, with this hospitality comes the responsibility of their protection. At this point in the story we might momentarily respect Lot. But then he pleads with the men outside, saying, "I beg you, my brothers, do not act so wickedly (Gen. 19:7)." We should feel uncomfortable with Lot addressing the men of Sodom as 'brothers', not of course in the familial sense, but in the sense of brethren, that is friends, associates, companions with whom you are in daily contact, with whom you might share a similar outlook on life. But this suggested bond between Lot and the men of Sodom could be dismissed by considering that Lot may simply have been using a polite form of address to appease the ever-pressing, lustful crowd. The shocking detail is rather in the next words to come forth from Lot's mouth:

> *Look, I have two daughters who have not known a man; let me bring them out to you and do to them as you please; only do nothing to these men, for they have come under the shelter of my roof.* (Gen. 19:8)

Hospitality and extending one's protection to houseguests is admirable, but Lot's graciousness has gone well beyond the call of duty. Offering his daughters to this insatiable crowd is unforgivable. Perhaps

Lot knew the men would not accept his offer, for they did not want his daughters, they desired the two male guests. Lot's character has indeed suffered a mighty blow. How could a father offer his two daughters to an entire city of men clearly for sexual abuse?[53] Conventional wisdom would say that Lot was trying to protect his two divine messengers; however, two divine messengers can certainly take care of themselves, as they did.

The story continues: the Sodomites charge the door, the men inside with not a moment to spare, pull Lot back into the safety of his house. Blindness strikes the Sodomites, preventing any further attempts to attack Lot's guests. At this point our story returns to the familiar. Lot, his wife and daughters prepare to flee the oncoming destruction of this wicked city. The story does not end here. It does not end with Lot's wife being turned into a pillar of salt.

As the story continues, not only will our respect for Lot continue to waiver, but our sympathies for his daughters will also be called into question. Lot left the region of Sodom and Gomorrah, as the text says, "for he was afraid to stay in Zoar (= region of these cities)." (Gen. 19:30) He went up into the hills that flank the region around the Dead Sea and there settled with his two daughters in a cave. This text provides us with an element of geographical credibility, for, as any traveler to this region knows, the Dead Sea is the lowest place on earth. Around it the topography is a hilly, rugged, dry and desolate region dotted with caves. Among these caves were discovered in modern times the Dead Sea Scrolls; among these caves in ancient times Jewish zealots sought shelter from the oncoming Roman legions. When we read the line "so he lived in a cave with his two daughters," it is as if we have reached a sad, lonely, desolate ending to our story. After the ghastly destruction by fire and brimstone, the ending is not only anti-climatic, but the imagery is the antithesis of what we experienced in the language and imagery of the text. We had the bustling, pressing, mobs of men in those wicked cities. Cities we envision as noisy, overcrowded, dirty, dusty, alive with who knows what activities, not only from sunup till sundown, but from sundown till sunup. Contrast that imagery with the present scene—Lot and his two daughters living alone in a small cave tucked into the cliffs. A sense of extraordinary desolation and quietness settles upon us.

Judean Wilderness beside the Dead Sea

With this closing we witness the extreme opposite of all that Sodom and Gomorrah represents. Or so we think—for the story goes on.

> *And the firstborn said to the younger, 'Our father is old and there is not a man on earth to come in to us after the manner of all the world. Come, let us make our father drink wine, and we will lie with him, so that we may preserve offspring through our father.'* (Gen. 19:31-32)

They follow through with their plan:

> So they made their father drink wine that night; and the firstborn went in, and lay with her father; he did not know when she lay down or when she rose.(Gen. 19:33)

If we are not yet uncomfortable with this story, we will be:

On the next day, the firstborn said to the younger, 'Look, I lay last night with my father; let us make him drink wine tonight also; then you go in and lie with him, so that we may preserve offspring through our father.' (Gen. 19:34)

Once again they follow through with their plan:

So they made their father drink wine that night also; and the younger rose, and lay with him; and he did not know when she lay down or when she rose. (Gen. 19:35)

The result of these incestuous relations was that both daughters became pregnant by their father and each bore a son:

The firstborn bore a son, and named him Moab; he is the ancestor of the Moabites to this day. The younger also bore a son and named him Ben-ammi; he is the ancestor of the Ammonites to this day. (Gen. 19:37-38)

As with most Hebrew names, the names of these sons carry an underlying meaning. Through minor creative philological adjustment the eldest daughter's son, named Moab, means 'from [the] father' (Hebrew *me'ab*); Ben-ammi, the son of the younger daughter, means 'son of my people' (Hebrew *ben-ammi*), clearly a euphemism that does not blatantly express the child was born of an incestuous relationship. Both sons are the eponymous (legendary) ancestors of a people; Moab became the Moabites and Ben-Ammi, the Ammonites, two peoples who will later inhabit the land on the other side of the Jordan River, the TransJordan, from the mid- to northern limits of the Dead Sea.

While this story may repulse us it does serve a purpose. It provides us with the origin of the eponymous ancestors of two nations that would inhabit the land beside the land promised to Abraham and his descendants. It also informs us that Moab and Ammon and their descendants are related to Abraham through his nephew Lot and are thus also related to the Israelites, the descendants of Abraham's grandson Jacob (=Israel).

The explicit connection of the Moabites in particular will be essential to later biblical history. In the period of the Judges, that volatile time when the tribes of Israel were attempting to settle into their new land, a young Moabite widow named Ruth will marry an Israelite from Bethlehem of Judah, named Boaz, and they will have a son named Obed. Obed is none other than the grandfather of King David who will forge the tribes of Israel into a mighty nation, a nation that will be expanded to empire-status by his most famous son, Solomon.

The Moabites, crucial for the future royal line of Israel, are also a proverbial thorn in her side. Earlier, when the Israelites attempt to enter the Promised Land via the TransJordan, King Balak of Moab will hire the seer Balaam to pronounce curses on Israel. Much to King Balak's surprise on each occasion for which he requests a curse against Israel, Balaam delivered an exquisite blessing on Israel and in the end the curse which Balak so desired came to rest upon his own head. After this series of blessings, rather than thanking Balaam and God, the Israelites let their lustful desires get the better of them and fall prey to wanton sexual acts with the Moabite women and honor of the Moabite god Baal Peor. Israel will be duly punished (Numbers 22-25).

Later, when Israel conquered the Promised Land and attempted to settle this new country, King Eglon of Moab will rise up and oppress Israel, moving across the Jordan and taking possession of the region in which the city of Jericho lies. Israel will remain under the domination of Moab for eighteen years until the charismatic Israelite judge Ehud assassinates Eglon and pushes the Moabites back across the Jordan (Judges 3:12-30). About two hundred years later, another king from Moab, King Mesha, will once again come calling against Israel, massacring thousands of Israelites in this same area, and again resettling Moabites in the former Israelite habitations. Moab at this time was particularly known for its worship of the god Chemosh, a god who required child sacrifice, a god who received as a sacrifice, King Mesha's own son (2 Kings 3). This is the nature of the Moabites, descended from the son born from the incestuous relations of Lot and his eldest daughter.

The Ammonites, though not as crucial to the future royal line of biblical history, play an antagonistic role in the history of Israel. During the period of the Judges, the Ammonites are one of the Canaanite peoples who remained after Joshua's conquest. They remained and oppressed the Israelites who lived in the region of Gilead in the northern TransJordan. For eighteen years they oppressed this region as well as crossing the Jordan and fighting against the tribes of Judah and Benjamin who had settled in the adjacent regions (Judges 10). It was the judge Jephthah who rose up and put down their oppression, but at the cost of the life of his only daughter (Judges 11:29-40).

The most famous episode, however, occurs towards the end of the period of the Judges, when Israel is struggling to remove pockets of Canaanite resistance that remained after the conquest by Joshua. One people who proved an insurmountable obstacle were the Philistines located in the southern coastal plain of Israel. Because of their threat Israel, still a coalition of tribes, eventually demands a stronger, more unified form of government, that of kingship. At the same time comes another threat, the Ammonites. The Ammonites, like the Moabites, dwelt in the TransJordan, in the northernmost area, north of Moab. When the Philistines hit Israel from the southwest, the Ammonites took advantage of Israel's plight and struck from the northeast. As was indicative during the period of the Judges, a charismatic military leader, called a judge, arose in Israel and delivered Israel from the oppressive Ammonites. This leader was none other than the judge who would become the first tentative king over Israel, Saul (1 Samuel 11).

Saul was a military man; he rose to the occasion by saving the men of Jabesh-gilead, a town in the northeastern regions of ancient Israel where Ammon struck the hardest. Ammon would permit only one form of surrender, a gesture that would indicate Israel's inferiority, Israel's subjugation and Israel's imperfection—every man must pluck out his right eye. The terms of surrender were inhumane; Saul rallied the tribes against Ammon, demonstrating his charisma. His victory pushed Ammon back across the Jordan and brought Saul into position as the first king of Israel.

Later during the reign of perhaps the greatest and most famous biblical king, David, Ammon would join the Aramaean league against Israel. In doing so, she would lose her independence when the league fell to David and become part of the empire of David, sending tribute as a sign of her subservience. Her independence would be regained, however, when the United Monarchy fell apart at the death of King Solomon. Ammon would then return to the Aramaean coalition and torment the two divided kingdoms of Israel and Judah. But Ammon and Moab would receive their due punishment when the great kingdom of Assyria would march in from the east and devastate all the kingdoms in her way to the Mediterranean Sea in the eighth century BC.

While we may recognize the literary and historical significance of the presence of the Moabites and the Ammonites in Israel's history, their necessity "to be" does not soften or make us less uncomfortable with the way they came into existence. Ancient commentators, too, expressed uneasiness with this story. Some Rabbinic texts (*BR* 51.8; PR 42.176a), the Church Fathers (Ephraim and Jerome), and Josephus (*AJ* I,11.4) all relate that the daughters believed they and their father were the only human beings left on earth, thus the daughters actions were essential to the continuation of the human race. Josephus quite simply states:

> *But his daughters, thinking that all mankind were destroyed, approached their father, though taking care not to be perceived. This they did, that humankind might not utterly fail.*

What is peculiar, however, is that both daughters bore sons, making the continuation of the human race impossible, lest incestuous relations are once again considered. With this thought in mind—perhaps—later Rabbinic commentators (Nachmanides, Rashi) dealt very harshly with Lot, viewing him as an incestuous father in the past.

In the end we *can* acknowledge that the Moabites and Ammonites are very much a part of biblical history. They are Israel's enemies, though they are all related. We *might* argue that marriage/relations to next-of-kin was an acceptable practice in the ancient world (consider the intermarriage in Egyptian royalty). We *might* argue that the biblical prohibition against relations with next-of-kin was not yet instigated (Lev. 18:6). We *might* even justify the actions of Lot and his daughters by noting that Moses excludes Ammonites and Edomites from being admitted to the assembly of the Lord—not because of their incestuous beginnings—but because they did not help Israel when she tried to enter the Promised Land and because they had hired Balaam to curse Israel (Deut. 23:3-6). We *might* forgive the 'act' because David is descended from the Moabites. But one question remains in my mind. Was a story of incest the only way to bring the Moabites and Ammonites into existence?

Leah of 'Dim' Eyes

"Laban had two daughters; the name of the elder was Leah, and the name of the younger was Rachel. Leah's eyes were dim but Rachel was graceful and beautiful" (Gen. 29:16-17). Leah's name means 'weary,' her eyes are described as *rakkhot* in Hebrew, a term that can be translated 'tender, soft or delicate'; the 'lovely' or 'dim' of some modern translations attempt to modify this adjective in its context.[54] It is not a compliment for it connotes immaturity in strength, weakness, or timidity. Rabbinic tradition, too, understood this implication when they wrote of Leah's poor eyesight.[55] By contrast, Rachel's name means 'ewe'; her description—graceful and beautiful—leaves no doubt that Jacob would be most impressed by her countenance and carriage.

And so it is Rachel that Jacob first beholds (Gen. 29:10), whom he kisses in greeting (29:11), the only woman to whom he expresses his love (29:18), and for whom he will serve her father Laban, his kinsman, for seven years in order to gain her hand in marriage (29:20). "And they [the seven years] seemed but a few days because of the love he had for her [Rachel]" (29:20). At the wedding feast Laban exchanges Rachel for Leah and beneath her bridal veil Leah's identity was hidden. Hidden until the morning light, when after consummating their marriage Jacob discovers the deception. "It was Leah!...What is this you [Laban] have done to me? Did I not serve with you for Rachel" resounds the voice of Jacob (29:25). Imagine how Leah felt, how Rachel felt, how Jacob felt. But Laban maintained the propriety of his ruse. Tradition dictated that the elder be married before the younger (29:26).

After the wedding week, Jacob was allowed to marry his beloved, Rachel, in exchange for another seven years of servitude to Laban. Imagine the joy of Rachel and Jacob, but what of Leah? The biblical text relates, "When the Lord saw that Leah was unloved, he opened her womb; but Rachel was barren" (29:31). Leah was fruitful; she would bear six sons for Jacob and one daughter.

First came **Reuben**, "Because the Lord **looked on** my affliction; surely now my husband will love me" (29:32). Then came **Simeon**, "Because the Lord has **heard** that I am hated, he has given me this son also" (29:33). And **Levi**, "Now this time my husband will be **joined** to me, because I have borne him three sons" (29:34). Each son's name was bestowed in accordance with her feelings (as in boldface).[56] But then came the fourth son and her pattern of naming changed, no longer did Leah seem to seek out the love or attention of Jacob. **Judah** was born and she said, "This time I will **praise** the Lord" (29:35). Leah *temporarily* ceased bearing.

Rachel, frustrated by her barrenness, "envied her sister" and lashed out at Jacob, "Give me children, or I shall die!" (30:1). Jacob responded with anger, "Am I in the place of God, who has withheld from you the fruit of the womb?" (30:2). Rachel's response was to give Jacob her handmaid Bilhah as a surrogate mother. And Bilhah bore two sons, **Dan**, "God has **judged** me [Rachel], and has also heard my voice and given me [Rachel] a son" (30:6) and **Naphtali**, "With mighty **wrestlings** I have **wrestled** with my sister, and have prevailed" (30:8). With the birth of two sons through a surrogate mother Rachel felt vindicated over Leah. But the competition continued.

Leah responded in kind, giving her handmaid, Zilpah, to Jacob to serve as a surrogate since she had ceased bearing children. And Zilpah bore **Gad** to Leah's comment, "**Good fortune!**" and **Asher**, "**Happy** am I [Leah]! For the women will call me happy!" (30:11,13).

And the competition continued. Leah's oldest son Reuben brought in mandrakes from the field for his mother. (Mandrakes were believed to impart fertility to the bearer.) Rachel pleaded with Leah for the mandrakes. Leah's response clearly indicted the strain between sisters, "Is it a small matter that you have taken away my husband? Would you take away my son's mandrakes also?" (30:15). Jacob returned from the field and spent the night with Leah, hired by virtue of the mandrakes. The mandrakes worked and Leah again conceived and bore a fifth son, **Issachar**, and Leah said, "God has given me my **hire** because I gave my maid to my husband" (30:19). And again Leah conceived, son number six, **Zebulun**, to which Leah exclaimed, "God has **endowed** me with a good dowry; now my husband will honor me, because I have borne him six sons" (30:20). And Leah also bore Jacob a daughter Dinah.

Finally, God remembered Rachel and she bore a son, **Joseph**, saying, "God has taken away my reproach…May the Lord **add** to me another son!" (30:23-24). Rachel does not sing out in thanks, but asks for another child! Later she would bear another son, Benjamin, with whom she would die in childbirth (35:18-19). Though Rachel and Jacob's earthly union ends, Rachel lives on through the prominence of her son Joseph and the devotion of Jacob to their son, Benjamin. Today, too, she is still remembered as visitors daily pay homage to this biblical matriarch at her tomb outside of Bethlehem.

But what of Leah's destiny? That she felt unloved by her husband is a given. That she is forgotten or her value diminished because of this lack of love would be most erroneous, ignoring her contribution to the future destiny of the nation Israel, in particular the royal line within Israel. Leah's first-born son, Reuben, will not bring this honor to his mother. Having slept with his father's concubine Bilhah, he is ostracized; his actions are construed of as one trying to usurp his father's authority (Gen. 35:22). Simeon and Levi, her second and third born, will also not add a sparkle to her eyes, for both are duly chastised for their actions of vengeance against the Shechemites when Shechem, their prince, violated their sister Dinah (Gen. 34).

Leah's fourth son, Judah, however, at whose birth Leah praised the Lord, is the one who will bring happiness and a sparkling glimmer to Leah's eyes. His son Perez will beget Hezron, Hezron will beget Ram,

Ram Amminadab, Amminadab Nahson, Nahson Salma, Salma Boaz, Boaz will beget Obed who will beget Jesse, the father of David. David, most esteemed king of Israel, of whom it is said "a star shall come out of Jacob, the scepter shall rise of Israel" (Numb. 24:17). David is this star, this scepter. David, born of the line of Leah and Jacob will forge the sons of Jacob, now tribes, into a United Monarchy. When David's United Monarchy of Israel is divided after the death of his son Solomon, it is Judah's name that is given to the Southern Kingdom (where Jerusalem and the Temple were located), while that of Israel (=Jacob) is bestowed on the Northern Kingdom.

The Northern Kingdom of Israel will be taken into captivity and be dispersed throughout the Middle East by the Assyrians in the 8th century BC. These ten tribes of Israel will forever be lost; Judah, however, will remain as the Southern Kingdom, absorbing into itself what remained of the little tribe of Benjamin (descendants of Rachel's son). Judah will be taken into Exile by the Babylonians in the 6th century BC, but permitted to return under the Persians in the 5th century BC and rebuild Israel. Judah will be remembered in the Greco-Roman designation of the Holy Land as Judea.

It is Leah's son Judah, too, whose name will forever be remembered (via Hebrew to Greek to Latin to Old French to English) in the designation Judaism and its adherents the Jews. All this began with the biblical matriarch, Leah of 'dim' eyes. Perhaps we should reconsider the translation of 'dim,' opting for its connotation of immaturity. Leah of immature vision became Leah of great vision when she blessed the Lord at the birth of her fourth son, Judah.

"Do Not Reject Your Mother's Teaching?!": The Role of Micah's Mother in Judges 17

Introduction

The first female figure in the book of Judges is a young woman named Achsah. As her story ends we find her riding upon donkey back to her father Caleb's home to request springs of water. These springs would allow her to sustain her new household on the fringe of the Negeb. The closing of her narrative brings thoughts of optimism to the reader regarding the future of her household and for Israel (Josh. 15:13-19; Judg. 1:10-15). The book of Judges closes with the story of another woman, the unnamed Levite's concubine. At the end of her story, she, like Achsah, journeys by donkey back to her master's house, but there is no optimism reflected in her ride, for it is her raped, abused and lifeless body that hangs over the donkey as the Levite brings her home (Judg. 19). Achsah's story represents the apex of Israel's vision and expectations for her future in the Promised Land; the story of the Levite's concubine is the nadir.

Between apex and nadir we find a prolific procession of female characters.[57] "How precisely, do the women of Judges fit into this overall picture of decline?" posits Danna Nolan Fewell in *The Women's Bible Commentary*. Her response is succinct, "The construction and destruction of female characters and their relationship form a pattern that mirrors the deterioration of Israel's relation to Yahweh."[58] Amidst this downward spiral of female characters, is the nameless mother of Micah, a woman who is deceptively constructed as a virtuous mother, only to be instantaneously deconstructed by a few choice words. Her unexpected deconstruction is paralleled by a 'deterioration of Israel's relation to Yahweh' in the private sphere of family worship.

Her story is found in Judges 17:1-4, a scene which serves as the Prologue to a larger narrative unit extending throughout Chapters 17 and 18. These chapters, along with Chapters 19-21, form a supplement to the book of Judges and have been extensively analyzed in respect to text-critical issues, their place in the textual history of the book of Judges,[59] and their function, especially in relation to cultic matters,[60] within the book of Judges and the Deuteronomic History.[61] The concern of the present paper is rather (1) the function of Micah's mother in Judges 17-18; (2) how her actions contribute to our understanding of the 'mother-son' relationship *and* the cultus in the book of Judges; and finally (3) how her actions foreshadow future perspectives on the introduction of idolatry in the Deuteronomic History. These concerns will be addressed by taking a literary approach with particular focus on the characterization of mother and son as presented through their actions, dialogue, narrator comments, and irony, that incongruity that will become apparent in the characterization of Micah and his mother. *Caveat lector!* The present story is an exception to the proverbial saying: *"Hear, my child, your father's instruction, and do not reject your mother's teaching; for they are a fair garland for your head, and pendants for your neck"* (Prov. 1:8).

The Story

"There was a man in the hill country of Ephraim whose name was Micayehu." So begins our story in Judges 17:1. We are immediately introduced to our protagonist Micayehu/Micah,[62] a man whose name meaning 'Who is like the Lord' portents great expectations for the reader. Our expectations will not be realized; he is not like the Lord, he

"Do Not Reject Your Mother's Teaching?!": The Role of Micah's Mother in Judges 17

is '*a* man,' "a man from the hill country of Ephraim," a designation that emphasizes his ordinary nature. This ordinariness subtly suggests what is about to transpire could very well happen to any man in Israel. The events about to transpire occur in 'the hill country of Ephraim,' a popular setting for the heroic stories of Deborah, Gideon, Abimelech, Tola, Jephthah, and Samuel and the following unfortunate episodes involving the Levite's concubine, Eli and Saul. In particular, the heroic nature of the preceding stories set in 'the hill country of Ephraim,' might by inference lead the reader into this same set of expectations, a complacency that our story will be once again follow the script of victorious combat.

In verse two we meet Micah's mother, designated simply as 'his mother' in the clause "He said to his mother." Nameless, our only expectations come from our preconceptions of what the term 'mother' evokes. Our narrator then begins *in media res* with a dialogue between son and mother, a dialogue that will be interrupted by narrator's comments. In verse two Micah says to his mother,

> "The eleven hundred pieces of silver that were taken from you, about which you uttered a *curse*, and even spoke it in my hearing, that silver is in my possession; I took it."

Her response is the converse, "May my son be *blessed* by the Lord!" 'What is taken,' the narrator relates, is returned in verse three: "Then he returned the eleven hundred pieces of silver to his mother." Once again and for the last time 'mother' speaks: "I *consecrate* the silver to the Lord from my hand for my son." For what purpose? For the antithesis of Israel's covenental law, "to make *an idol of cast metal*; (*pesel umassekah*)."[63] The narrator relates the completion of events in verse four:

> So when he returned the money to his mother, his mother took two hundred pieces of silver, and gave it to the silversmith, who made it into an idol of cast metal; and it was in the house of Micah.

We then read the narrator's summary in verse five,[64] followed by a familiar refrain in verse six:

> This man Micah had a shrine, and he made an ephod and teraphim, and installed one of his sons who became priest. In those days there was no king in Israel, all the people did what was right in their own eyes.

Micah's story will continue in Chapters 17 and 18, his mother will disappear. He will acquire a Levite to replace his son as priest in his shrine. The idol and the Levite will be taken unexpectedly by the Danites as they migrate northwards. Micah and his entourage, being no match for the Danite force, will relinquish the idol and the Levite. The Danites will move on to take the unsuspecting Canaanite city of Laish, rename it Dan, and establish the ancient cultic center of Dan. Our focus, however, is on what can be discerned, both stated and implied, from the initial dialogue and narrator comments in respect to our characters, their relationship, and how this information contributes to our understanding of the cultus in its immediate and extended context.

Characterization and Irony

Of mother we learn that she had 1100 pieces of silver, whether this amount makes her affluent has been much debated; however, in verse ten Micah offers the Levite ten pieces of silver as a yearly wage, suggesting 1100 pieces may be a significant amount. No mention is made of her husband, Micah's father, which by inference might suggest she was a widow, an affluent widow at that. She would belong to that class of women so often deemed among the lowliest of Israel, "the widow, the orphan and the sojourner." Her affluence contradicts our usual expectations of the poor widow in biblical literature.

On learning of her loss, we as readers may initially be sympathetic. Her utterance of a curse is excusable, reflecting a natural human response. On discovering that her son Micah is the thief, our compassion is extended further toward 'mother.' Our esteem for the nameless mother rises, when, as a sign of forgiveness, she blesses her son, the thief.[65] The altruistic nature of 'mother' peaks as we learn that the very money stolen from her will now be consecrated to the Lord. But the esteem we hold for this mother will instantly be lost when we learn of the purpose of the consecrated money—"to make an idol of cast metal (*pesel umassekah*) on behalf of my son." Her character is further tainted when we learn that of the 1100 pieces of consecrated silver only 200 are given to the silversmith. Was this amount his fee? Or did she add insult to transgression by holding back some of the consecrated money? The answer lies is conjecture.

Micah's mother, as noted, speaks but twice. Ironically, both utterances drawn from the parlance of cultic activity—a formula of blessing and an act of consecration—yield the antithesis of covenantal law. In particular she breaks the Second Commandment "You shall not make for yourself an idol (*pesel*)..." (Exod. 20:4) and admonitions found in Lev. 19:4,11. The use of the term *massekah* also evokes allusions to Exod. 32 where *massekah* is the term used of the Golden Calf. (Ironically, in Rabbinic literature Micah is charged with having fashioned the Golden Calf.) The conjoining of these two terms certainly adds negative connotations to the one who commissioned it—Micah's mother.

But son Micah is by no means virtuous. He openly admits his thievery; breaking not only the Eighth Commandment "Thou shalt not steal," but in stealing from his mother he also transgresses the Fifth Commandment "Honor your father and your mother." Why he chose to return the silver may derive more from the fear of his mother's curse,[66] which the text is specific to note was pronounced in his hearing, than from feelings of guilt or remorse. Youthful folly cannot be held responsible for his crime, for in verse five we learn that he has sons, one of whom is old enough to be initiated as the priest of his shrine. We might also posit the question, "What kind of role model does Micah as father serve for his own sons?" Is Micah an exemplar of our proverb *"Hear, my child, your father's instruction!"*?

Micah not only breaks two major commandments, but by willingly accepting the idol from his mother he, like his mother, breaks the Second as well "You shall not bow down to them or worship them." In her discussion of the book of Judges in *A Women's Bible Commentary*, Fewell quizzes "What kind of mother leads her son into idolatry?"[67] What Fewell and other commentators fail to note is that the son, Micah, willingly accepts the introduction of idolatry. He is no more coerced into idolatry than Adam was coerced to eat of the fruit of the tree by Woman. All had free will.

The actions of Micah as thief and 'mother' as commissioner of an idol create uncomfortable feelings for the reader. But it is our knowledge that the inappropriate actions of both are directed against one another AND more importantly that the relationship between characters is the *most nurturing* of family relationships, that of 'mother-child,' that turns discomfort to shock for the reader. It is none other than irony, that unexpected reversal of tantalizing expectations of a son named Micah and 'his mother' that makes our story so intriguing and so appropriate to its volatile social setting in the period of the Judges. Micayehu "Who is like the Lord," is certainly not "like the Lord." Micah, a son, a father, is a thief, a profession no parent wishes for their child. He is neither a blessing to his mother, nor a role model for his sons. Mother, a widow (?), the image of the oppressed, is wealthy and certainly not the apotheosis of 'mother'; her teachings—idolatry—are certainly not 'fair garland or pendants for adornment.' The characterization of Micah and mother reflect the deconstruction of this most special parental bond. Placed in the context of other 'mother-child' relationships in the biblical text, an even more poignant image of deterioration obtains. No other mother-son relationship depicts such outright disrespect of child for parent or parent for child.

Contrast yielding irony, however, is not restricted to the character and relationship of our protagonists, but is inherent in the vocabulary of the Prologue of Chapter 17 and in the ensuing events. Silver is taken (*lqh*) and returned (*shwb*); mother utters a curse (*'alyt*), then a blessing (*berakhah*); covenantal law is acknowledged by a blessing (*berakhah*) and a consecration (*haqdesh heqdashti*) to the Lord, then wantonly broken by the antithesis of covenantal law, the commissioning of an idol (*pesel umassekah*). All the silver is consecrated to the Lord, but then part is withheld. Micah's non-Levitical son is installed as priest, using the very language for the ordination of the Levites (Exod. 28:41; Lev.8:27) and then replaced by an official Levite; the Levite who had been a sojourner, is asked to settled down with Micah; Micah finds security in his idol and the Levite, but then loses his security to the Danites. Characterization, vocabulary and ensuing events all yield irony.

Of all contrasts, however, it is the contrast in dialogue, or better the break in dialogue, that is most pronounced and destructive to our perception of family and family cultic life during this period. We saw that Micah's admission of thievery was countered by his mother's words of blessing (v. 2)—son spoke, mother responded; but mother's consecration of silver to the Lord on behalf of her son for a molten idol was countered by silence. Acquiescence by silence speaks louder than any words. No refusal is forthcoming from Micah—mother spoke, son did not verbally respond. Micah's silent acceptance is confirmed by the narrator at the end of verse four with the words "and it [the molten idol] was in the house of Micah," *and* in verse five when the narrator summarizes "this man Micah had a shrine and HE MADE an ephod and teraphim, and installed one of his sons, who became priest." Mother commissioned the idol; son not only maintained the idol, but installed a priest and added cultic accoutrements.

The narrative in all its detail has enticed the reader into one set of expectations, but ever so quickly and ever so subtly our expectations have been deconstructed by incongruity. It is this very incongruity that makes the reader realize that what we expected of family and cult towards the end of the period of the Judges is not what we obtained;

however, these perspectives may indeed represent a glimpse of what Israelite society was like. As readers we have to determine whether our episode was preserved because it is paradigmatic of similar households, relationships and cultic activity at this time, or whether our story is an exception, demonstrating what might occur or continue to occur if Israelite society does not make changes in her political, social and religious spheres.

Beyond the Immediate

Contrast within the story of Micah and his mother provides a striking example of the breakdown of this most precious parental relationship. Perhaps the sanctity of the mother-son relationship is what led Rabbinic commentators to give a name to our nameless mother of Micah—Delilah.[68] While the connection of Micah's mother with Delilah may be the product of legend, the equation is tantalizing.[69] Admonitions against the power and influence of foreign women, be they wives, mothers or seductresses are not uncommon in the Hebrew Bible.[70] In Rabbinic thought Micah's mother as a foreigner, specifically as Delilah, may soften the harshness of the breakdown of the 'mother-son' relationship; making the initiator of idolatry a foreign woman may lessen the severity of the sin. It is not an Israelite mother who introduces idolatry and gets her Israelite son to willingly follow, it is a foreigner—it is Delilah!

Micah's mother as Delilah may be the product of fanciful speculation by early Rabbinic schools, but behind their imaginings may lie a perspective that serves to connect our story with what precedes and follows. Polzin argued that "a particular passage 'makes sense' if it repeats compositional patterns already encountered in what precedes it and foreshadows perspectives that lie ahead."[71] Robert Alter noted, "the matrix of allusion is often a sense of absolute historical continuity and recurrence, or an assumption that earlier events and figures are timeless ideological models by which all that follows can be measured."[72]

In its immediate context, the story of Micah and his mother makes sense because it illustrates specific spheres in which Israelite society has deteriorated, namely the character of widow, mother, son, the mother-son relationship and religion. In serving as the Prologue, it naturally provides the necessary background details and the initial conflict that will unfold in the remainder of Chapter 17 and into Chapter 18. Beyond the immediate context, our attention may first be drawn to comparison of our 'mother-son' relationship with 'mother-son' relationships that precede; however, most intriguing is the cultic activity represented in our story. It is in reference to this topic that our story can indeed 'make sense' in what has preceded and what will follow. In addressing this topic the most difficult obstacle is determining the nature of the cultus as inferred by the events in our Prologue.

Most commentators and scholars of Israelite religion view our passage as an example indicating that personal family shrines were a common feature of Israelite religion during the period of the Judges.[73] Gerstenberger goes so far as to see in our story "a later echo of the original clan religion." He poses many penetrating questions regarding the nature of this family shrine.[74] Unfortunately, he does not answer the most telling question of all? Does the molten idol represent Yahweh or a pagan god? Within the context of the period of the Judges another response to his unanswered question may be found. After the death of Joshua, the book of Judges (2:10-13) speaks of Israel's severed relationship with the Lord of their ancestors. A new generation grew up who did not know the Lord, they worshipped the Baal and the Astartes, and they abandoned the Lord. Throughout the period of the Judges, Israel confronted with the Canaanite religion, gives in to paganism. But Israel apparently did not wholly abandon the Lord, for it is to Him that she will repeatedly cry when suffering the oppression of those Canaanites who were not displaced in the Conquest. Micah's domestic shrine may be influenced by the Canaanite culture around her, more so than a reflection or echo of the patriarchal clan religion. But more importantly Micah and mother's story might also reflect an early, if not the earliest, example of religious syncretism of Yahwism and the Canaanite culture. Belief in Yahweh and possession of pagan objects coexist in Micah's story: Micah's name evokes Yahwistic connections, his mother's speech evokes Yahwistic connections; mother's commissioning of a molten idol indicates pagan connections, Micah's acceptance of these articles indicates pagan connections. Acceptance of both Yahwism and paganism might suggest syncretism was present in domestic shrines during the period of the Judges.[75]

The intrusion of idolatry (possibly syncretism) into the cultus provides a thematic link between our story and those stories depicting the state of the cultus later in the Deuteronomic History. So, for example, we find echoes of details from Micah's story in I Kings 12 where Jeroboam, the first king of the Northern Kingdom builds his first capital Shechem located in none other than the hill country of Ephraim. Jeroboam goes on to establish the shrines of Bethel and Dan, each with a golden calf. He also sets us high places with non-Levitical priests. His mother, a widow, is mentioned by name, Zeru'ah. But it is not just the continuity of these details that allows our story to 'make sense,' rather it is the gender relations depicted in our story in relation to the intrusion of idolatry that provides a unique and dynamic link with the Deuteronomic history. While gender knows no distinction in its support of Yahwism or paganism—Micah and his mother are equal advocates of both—it is Micah's mother who initiates idolatry and Micah who willingly accepts and officiates over the shrine. Thus it is woman who initiates and man who officiates. It is this compositional pattern of woman and idolatry that is repeated in the Deuteronomic History to follow.

In I Kings 11:1 we learn that "Solomon loved many foreign women" and his wives turned away his heart after other gods (11:4f). In I Kings 14:21 Rehoboam son of Solomon came to reign over Judah; his mother is Naamah the Ammonite. During his reign Judah did what was evil in the sight of the Lord. In I Kings 15:12 King Asa of Judah removed his mother from her regal position as queen mother because she made an image for Asherah. But the text also adds that Asa did not remove the high places though his heart was still to the Lord (15:14). In I Kings 16:31 Ahab of Israel takes Jezebel, daughter of Ethbaal of the Sidonians as wife. With Jezebel we have the apotheosis of foreign woman transmitting the evils of paganism. In II Kings 8:25 Jehoram of Judah comes to the throne. His mother was Athaliah, a granddaughter of King Omri of Israel. The text is specific to note that Jehoram walked in the 'way of the house of Ahab…for he was son-in-law to the house of Ahab' (II K 8:27). On the death of her son Jehoram, Athaliah destroys the rest of the royal family, save one son, Joash, who is spirited away by the priest Jehoiada. Athaliah will subsequently be put to death (II K 11:16), at which time a new covenant is made between the Lord, the king and the people; and notably pagan elements are purged from the land (II K 11:17f).[76] II Chronicles 22:3 is specific to note that Athaliah was Jehoram's counselor in acting wickedly.

In the subsequent annals of the Kings of Judah and Israel as related in the book of Kings, we find eighteen of the twenty introductory formulas for the Kings of Judah specifically mention the mother's name after the father. Excluding Hezekiah (II K 18) and Josiah (II K 22) the text notes that none of the kings completely walked in the way of the Lord, most at the very least allowed the high places to remain.[77] If only we could make a similar connection with these mothers and the presence of idolatry, a further connection with Micah's mother would obtain. If mother in our story is the initiator of idolatry and this association convincingly continues in the Deuteronomic History, blame for religious indiscretion can be subtly directed by the male hand toward woman. If the woman is foreign—as the Rabbis saw in Micah's mother, as the text states with Solomon's wives and in particular in his successor Rehoboam's Ammonite mother—the guilt can also be directed away from Israelite women to foreign woman.[78]

Final Thoughts

Whether or not Micah's mother is foreign, she is present in this biblical narrative. We did not need her in this story. Our narrative might just as well have begun with a modification of the narrator's summary in verse five:

> There was a man named Micah who lived in the hill country of Ephraim. He had a shrine with an idol. He made an ephod and teraphim, and installed one of his sons who became his priest.

But she is a woman present in a male-dominated narrative; she needs to be acknowledged and explained. She is not marginal, peripheral or incidental in her relationship to her son or to the confines of the Prologue. The ramifications of her actions extend beyond the Prologue. As a mother whose actions interact with the family cultus, we are compelled to compare her with other biblical mothers and the state of the cultus throughout the biblical narrative. It is her actions with regard to the cultus that give us an inauspicious impression of her as mother, an impression that contradicts our past perceptions of mother and may very well unjustly influence our future perceptions of a biblical mother, in particular when mother comes into contact with the cultus, by her actions or by her mere presence in a narrative that speaks of the cultus.

The story of Micah, his idol and his further adventures with the tribe of Dan is most often remembered as a narrative that depicts the negative origin of the great cultic center of Dan. It is a story that "has become a polemic piece in the Deuteronomic compilation."[79] Until now Micah's mother has scarcely been noted as playing any part in this narrative. Given her unfavorable role, perhaps contemporary women might wish she had been left in the shadows of her son Micah. But in reintroducing her to contemporary society we must not be impolite and now neglect her son Micah who willingly *'did not reject his mother's teachings.*

Mrs. Job

In the book of Job we find the tale of a righteous man who is brought to suffer as a backdrop for debating such issues as theodicy, unjust suffering, suffering in general, the grandeur of God in creation and the nature of wisdom.[80] We are taught to focus on these issues rather than on the precise details of the folkloric story (that frames this epic poem) of the 'patient' Job who loses his possessions and his children, and then is physically brought to suffer. As readers, however, we do have the inside tract; we know that Job suffers in vain, that his children are taken as part of this horrible wager between God and the prosecuting *ha-satan* "the adversary" in the heavenly court. We cannot forget this information as we struggle through the tumultuous cycles of speeches with his friends Eliphaz, Bildad and Zophar, as each friend tries to make Job confess his guilt. The equation is simple: suffering = guilty. But we as readers know he is innocent. We do not forget.

We also should not forget Job's wife. We meet her in Chapter 2. Job has already suffered the loss of oxen, donkeys, sheep, camels, servants, and seven sons and three daughters. Job has delivered his most classic response: "Naked I came from my mother's womb, and naked I shall return there; the Lord giveth, the Lord taketh away: Blessed be the name of the Lord" (Gen. 1:21). Job has now become afflicted with odious sores as he sits on an ash-heap on the outskirts of the city, scraping his sores with a potsherd. And then his wife—she has not yet been mentioned—speaks—the first and only time: "Do you still persist in your integrity? Curse God and die" (Job 2:10). His response is again a classic quote of patience indicative of the folkloric story (Job 1-2, 42):

"You speak as one of the foolish women would speak. Shall we receive the good at the hand of God, and not receive the bad?" (Job 2:10). In the Hebrew text, Job's wife literally says "Bless God and die!" Bless is understood as a scribal emendation to avoid the text literally stating the blasphemous, "Curse God and die!" But the meaning is clear. Job's wife is asking him to commit 'suicide' by blaspheming God; God would strike him dead, putting an end to his misery. Rabbinic tradition tries to soften this statement by noting that Job's wife was not sure of his steadfastness; immediate death was the only recourse.[81] Of her fate we are not told; why she was spared we are not told. We assume, or perhaps have given it no thought at all, that she is the same wife who will bear Job seven more sons and three more daughters at the end of our story when Job's patience is rewarded with greater wealth and a new family.

The Greek translation of the *Hebrew Bible*, called the *Septuagint*, however, did not forget Job's wife nor does an extra-biblical text called *The Testament of Job*. Both texts acknowledge that Job's wife, too, suffered. She carried and nurtured each of the ten children. Why wouldn't she be distraught? The quality of her life would have also changed with the loss of Job's possessions and it was *her* husband who was suffering. The Greek text acknowledges her feelings in its expansion at Job 2:9:

> *"And when much time had passed, his wife said to him, 'How long will you hold out, saying, Behold I wait yet a little while, expecting the hope of my deliverance? For behold, your memorial is abolished from the earth, your sons and daughters, the pangs and pains of my womb which I bore in vain with sorrows; and you yourself sit down to spend the nights in the open air among the corruption of worms, and I am a wanderer and a servant from place to place and house to house, waiting for the setting of the sun, that I may rest from my labors and my pangs which now beset me: but say some word against the Lord, and die'."*

In the extra-biblical work entitled *The Testament of Job*,[82] Job gathers his second group of children around him as he puts his affairs in order for his impending death. He relates to these children the events of his life and in doing so we learn further details about Job's background. He reminds them that he is from the seed of Esau, the brother of Jacob, but they are from the seed of Jacob because their mother was Jacob's daughter Dinah! Dinah according to this text and Rabbinic tradition is the second wife of Job. She was married to Job after being raped by the Canaanite prince Shechem (Gen. 38).

As for Job's first wife, she is given a name in the *Testament of Job*, Sitis. She *does not* survive Job's test of faith, which indeed is also her test. The *Testament* relates that she, like Job, suffered. Job, while sitting on his ash-heap with the plague, watched her carrying water as a maidservant to the home of noblemen—once Job's equals—just to earn bread to feed Job (Ch. 21). She continued in this way for eleven years, but then due to the harsh treatment of her 'masters' she was not able to bring any more food to Job; she had barely enough food for herself. Yet she would take her meager daily food and divide it in half to give Job some sustenance (Ch. 22). She even took to begging for bread to further nourish the ailing Job.

At this point Satan enters. In the *Testament*, Satan is the equivalent of the devil contrary to the biblical text where the term was used of a prosecuting member of God's heavenly court. Satan came disguised as a bread seller (Ch. 23). Having no money, she gave him the hair of her head for three loaves of bread. (According to the Talmud, the greatest sacrifice a wife could make was to support her husband by selling her hair.[83]) Satan followed her and "and led her heart astray" (23:11). It was Satan's work that led Sitis to recite her words of woe as found in the Greek text's expansion and in this work. In the *Testament*, a lament for Sitis follows, drawing even sharper the contrast between the quality of her present and past life. Then follows her request for Job to "Curse God and die!"; however, in this text she wishes that they both die. Job responds that her words hurt more than any of his losses. But he does acknowledge that Sitis, too, is suffering.

Sitis appears again in the *Testament*—after Job's lengthy discourse with his friends. She asks that his friends help her give proper burial to their children, still buried beneath the rubble of the collapsed building where they dined together. Job remarks that this is not necessary because they are already in heaven. He allows her to look toward the east and see them already in splendor with God. When she beholds this vision, she declares, "Now I know that I have a memorial with the Lord" (40:4). Her intent was then to return to the city and rest a while before returning to her servitude. She lay down in a cow shed "and died in good spirits" (40:6). When her ruler found her, she was "sprawled out dead" among the animals. Great lamentation arose over her death. She was carried in procession, buried near the house which had collapsed on her children. The poor of the city cried out in lament, "Look! This is Sitis, the woman of pride and splendor! She was not even considered worthy of a decent burial!" (40:13). Perhaps she did receive a 'decent burial,' for her final resting-place was beside that of her children.

When we read these traditions about Job's wife, we must remember that they are later traditions; they are not the biblical text. But they remind us that others, centuries ago, pondered the fate of Job's wife. In their reflections (or in the established traditions they were passing down) they wanted future generations to realize that Job's wife, too, suffered in her own right and should be accorded sympathy and remembrance for her endurance. We should think of her as more than an appendage to Job, more than the impetus that will inspire Job to expound pain through poetry, more than Mrs. Job.

Vashti... Who?

On that one particular late spring morning about two years ago, I knew of Vashti. I knew of her defiance to higher authority; I knew of the strength of her convictions; the sound of her defiant words echoed in my mind. But then again I had recently become re-acquainted with her in an adult education course I had taught.[84] I seem to recall also having made her acquaintance during my graduate studies while working as a research assistant.[85] What a bold, intriguing woman I had thought. Though overshadowed by her successor, once met she was hard to dismiss. Given the fame of her successor, I realized making her acquaintance might prove difficult for many people and so I could understand why participants in my adult education course were unfamiliar with Vashti. I could also understand the pause in Regis' voice that spring morning when Regis (of *Live with Regis and Kathie Lee*) took a call from a Vashti. He commented that the name was unfamiliar to him. Vashti explained that her father, affiliated with the ministry, had named her after a woman who appeared in the first chapter of the book of Esther. Though I knew of Vashti because of my teaching and research, I, like Regis, paused on hearing a caller named Vashti. Other biblical names are bestowed upon new-born baby girls, names like Sarah, Rebecca, Rachel, Leah, Dinah, Deborah, Miriam/Mary, Ruth, Naomi, and Esther—to name but a few, but Vashti! Or rather—why not Vashti? Why has Vashti been overlooked? Her story and related legends may provide a clue.

Vashti was queen to Ahasuerus, King of the Persian Empire, an empire that stretched from India to Ethiopia, preceding that of Greece and Rome. The time was approximately the early fifth century BC. Ahasuerus is most often associated with the Persian king Xerxes I (486-465BC), the son of Darius I Hystaspes (522-486BC). Darius was of the royal lineage of Cyrus the Great who overthrew another great kingdom, that of Babylon in 538BC, a kingdom which but fifty years earlier under Nebuchadnezzar had destroyed Jerusalem and the Temple and taken the people of Judah into Exile.[86] Vashti, according to Rabbinic legend, was the daughter of Belshazzar, the son of this very same Nebuchadnezzar, king of Babylon. Though daughter of a fallen monarch, as queen she filled a position of great dignity, which necessitated giving allegiance to her new emperor, her former enemy, her husband, Ahasuerus.[87]

As our story opens the narrator is very careful to detail the grandeur and affluence of Ahasuerus' kingdom. In his capital, Susa, the opening scene is carnivalesque, with banqueting for all of the officials, ministers and armies of Persia and Media. One hundred and eighty days of banqueting at this grand level are followed by a more private celebration for only those men of the capital city of Susa. This private banqueting lasts but seven days. The text richly details the lavishness of this banquet with great emphasis on "drinking...without restraint" (Esther 1:8). Queen Vashti follows the king's lead, giving a banquet for the women of the palace. The text is silent about what Vashti and her ladies did at their banquet. However, the Targum (Aramaic translation) adds that the ladies were talking about the king, especially about private matters and his quarters.

On the final day of feasting, the King commanded Vashti to be brought before him, wearing the crown, in order to show the people and the officials her beauty (1:11). Vashti refuses. Rabbinic literature states that when the biblical text says, "wearing the crown," it means 'wearing only the crown!' From Rabbinic legend we also learn that amidst the drunken banter of the king and his officials, they argue over which women were more beautiful: Babylonian, Median, or Persian. Ahasuerus claims of course that Vashti, the Babylonian, "the vessel which he is using" is of course the most beautiful. And then he asks, "Would you like to see her?"

Clearly this summons is degrading to Vashti. She is an object to be displayed before men who have been drinking for seven plus 180 days; she existed to entertain. We respect her sense of modesty and chastise the crude, boorishness of the king. In her marriage to her enemy, Vashti has already been humiliated as a spoil of war, but now to acquiesce to such an immodest request—regardless of how she was clothed—clearly goes beyond the call of political duty. Amidst this debauchery, Vashti maintains her dignity. She refuses! But at what expense?

Following Persian custom, the king consulted his seven top officials before issuing any decree when matters of state were threatened. Once an edict was enacted it could not be rescinded. Only a second edict could perhaps soften the harshness of the first. This defiance—which to us might seem trivial—is treated as monumental a threat as a major uprising in one of the provinces of the Empire. They advise the king that an edict must be issued "so that Vashti is never again to come before the king. And all women of all status are ordered to pay homage to their husbands" (1:19). They believe her action has threatened the dominance of every husband in the kingdom. Her action marks her as a threat to the status quo of Persian society, disrupting the social order.

The biblical text goes on to say, "Vashti is never again to come before the king" (1:19). It implies that she is deposed from her position of primary wife. Following Rabbinic legend, however, Vashti was executed. Later when the king's anger subsided—and we presume his drunken stupor—he remembered Vashti and his edict. His reaction is not one of shock or disbelief, but rather contrary to the grand description of his wealth and kingdom, the king is portrayed as a buffoon, an impotent ruler without control. Our sympathies are not with the king. He calls his seven top officials for advice. They suggest he must find a new queen. And a search or better a beauty contest of young virgins will follow. Vashti's defiance paves the way for the successful entrance of Esther who will eventually be chosen as the next queen and save the Jewish people in their exile.

Vashti disappears from the story. No further reference to Vashti is made in the Hebrew Bible. As a reader we may feel a sense of sympathy for this vanquished or executed Queen whom we have barely come to know; she briefly occupied our thoughts. Vashti never spoke a word; all details regarding her were reported by male characters. Vashti was given no voice. Modern feminist find disappointment in Vashti, not because of her actions, but because she disappears and is forgotten. There is no holiday celebrating her boldness and no remembrance of her self-sacrifice.[88]

We have no other biblical documentation to help us in our characterization of Vashti. However, if we look to Persian records for clues we will find reference to an Amestris, wife of Xerxes I. Her character is not flattering for history records that she had her niece mutilated and put to death for having an affair with her husband. Clearly such an offense was punishable by death; however, the manner in which she achieved 'justice' belies her brutality. At her husband Xerxes' birthday celebration she requested the brutal execution of her niece, his mistress. According to Persian law, a request at such an occasion must be honored. The king must acquiesce, issuing the decree with his very own lips.

Rabbinic legend, too, tries to present Vashti in a harsh light thereby alleviating any guilt over her removal and replacement by Esther. One tradition relates her fate came on the Sabbath as punishment for her habit of having Jewish maidens spin and weave on the Sabbath day, deprived of their clothing; another tells that it was Vashti who had prevented the king from rebuilding the Temple, which her ancestors had destroyed.

Literary and historical traditions, such as I have related, suggest that there may be more to the character of Vashti than presented in the Biblical text. But we must use these extra-biblical traditions with caution. The association of Queen Amestris with Vashti may be tempting, but the equation is not of certainty. Likewise Rabbinic legends may be just that, tales that add a wicked spice to the character of Vashti. We may be fascinated and influenced by their responses, but in the end we have to decide how to evaluate and understand the character of Vashti on the basis of the biblical text. Vashti, in Persian her name may mean "best." Her fate certainly was not the best. In the end we are left with a single poignant image of Vashti: she is bold, defiant and justifiably so, whether clad in only her crown or her crown with full regalia, as she adamantly maintains her stance and her convictions.

"Queen Vashti refused to come at the king's command conveyed by the eunuchs," records the Bible (Esther 1:12). "No! No! I will not do as you say? No, no, I will not compromise myself in any way!," sings the Vashti of Elizabeth Swados' musical *Bible Women*.[89] These are bold words that beg us to take notice. These are words for which Vashti should be remembered.

Oh, Susanna, Daniel Cried Out for Thee!

"Day after day they watched eagerly to see her...It was a hot day" and *Susanna "wished to bathe in the garden." "No one was there except the two elders, who had hidden themselves and were watching her. She said to her maids, 'Bring me olive oil and ointments, and shut the garden doors so that I can bathe."* And so her maids left the beautiful Susanna alone in the garden (Daniel 13:12,15-18).[90]

Susanna, her name means 'lily,' a reflection of her beauty—a trait that may very well be the cause of her forthcoming trial and tribulation. She was "trained according to the Law of Moses" (Dan. 13:3), which influenced, no doubt, her righteousness and reverence for God. Her husband Joakim ('the Lord is right') was a very affluent, honorable man. They lived in Babylon, home of the exiles from Judah, after Nebuchadnezzar had destroyed Judah in 587BC. Both came from prominent families, thus Joakim's home was a focal point for the community. To Joakim the Jews would come for advice; mornings elders who served as judges would adjudicate in his domicile. At noon, all visitors would depart and Susanna would go to the garden adjoining her home to stroll and reflect. Such was the daily routine of Joakim and Susanna's household. Susanna's routine was noted by two elders and "they began to lust for her"(Dan. 13:8). Though they tried to "suppress their consciences" and focus on "their duty to administer justice" (Dan. 13:9-10), "lustful desires" prevailed. Each judge, however, did not let the other know of his passion. They "watched" and "hid" in the garden—two verbs that will figure prominently in this private sphere.

Time moves rapidly forward. Once upon a time became that year which became every day, which became one day, but it was not just another day of voyeurism. On this day, after everyone had gone home, the two elders circled back separately to look upon the beauty of Susanna. Their lustful desires, however, were revealed when each discovered the presence of the other. They confessed their mutual lust for Susanna. Individual voyeuristic tendencies turned to a joint plan for an opportune afternoon "when they could find her alone" (Dan. 13:14). "Watching" eventually brought an opportune day. It was hot. Susanna followed her usual routine. She went to the garden; however, this time she "wished to bathe" so as to cool herself from the oppressive heat. The elders were once again hidden and watching. On this day she sent away her maids to fetch her toiletries. Once brought, they were to "shut the garden doors, so that she could bathe" (Dan. 13:17). And so they did.

The garden, her respite and refuge from the demands of her community, today was to be her respite and refuge from the heat. With doors shut Susanna was safe from the outside world. But out came the two elders, running towards her, in unison crying, "Look the garden doors are shut, and no one can see us" (Dan. 13:20). They who had been guilty of immoral 'seeing' are now concerned with being seen! They openly revealed their feelings to Susanna. It is not love but lust: "we are burning with desire for you! Give your consent, and lie with us" (Dan. 13:20). But there is more: "If you refuse, we will testify against you that a young man was with you, and this was why you sent your maids away" (Dan. 13:21).

The garden paradise of refuge now brought entrapment: "I am completely trapped. For if I do this, it will mean death for me; if I do not, I cannot escape your hands. I choose not to do it; I will fall into your hands, rather than sin in the sight of the Lord" (Dan. 13:22). "Fall into your hands"—if Susanna literally gives in to their desires she is guilty of the sin of adultery; if she refuses, their fallacious story will also lead to charges of adultery.[91]

Susanna's decision? Crying out with a LOUD voice, she threw herself into the hands of fate and God. Immediately the elders also shouted. Garden doors were flung open for all to 'see.' The entire household saw AND heard the vile tale of the elders. The servants' were ashamed, "for nothing had ever been said about Susanna" (Dan. 13:27). Did they believe this tale? The next day would tell. As on every other day, all gathered at Joakim's house for judgment. This time, however, it was the beautiful and virtuous Susanna who was on trial. The elders were there with their "wicked plot to have Susanna put to death" (Dan. 13:28).

Slowly a procession moved toward the assembly: Susanna, her parents, children and relatives. But where was her husband Joakim? Though she makes her appearance veiled, we as readers are reminded of her refinement and beauty. Does this intimate her guilt? "The scoundrels ordered her to be unveiled," not so that she could openly face her judgment, but because "they might feast their eyes on her beauty" (Dan. 13:32). The crowds wept openly, her relatives wept openly and tears blurred Susanna's eyes as she tilted her head toward heaven in prayer: "For she trusted in the Lord" (Dan. 13:35).

The vile tale was recounted:

> *"While we were walking in the garden alone, this woman came in with two maids, shut the garden doors, and dismissed the maids. Then a young man, who was hiding there, came to her and lay with her. We were in a corner of the garden and when we saw this wickedness we ran to them. Although we saw them embracing, we could not hold the man, because he was stronger then we, and he opened the doors and got away. We did, however, seize this woman and asked who the young man was, but she would not tell us. These things we testify"* (Dan. 13:36-41).

"These things we testify!" They were elders, judges; they were believed. Two esteemed witnesses against one woman. "The assembly condemned her to death" (Dan. 13:41). But Susanna cried out in a LOUD voice, just as she had cried out in the garden:

> *"O eternal God, you know what is secret and are aware of all things before they come to be; you know that these men have given false evidence against me. And now I am to die, though I have done none of the wicked things that they have charged against me!"* (Dan. 13:42-43).

The Lord heard her cry. The assembly did not recant their verdict. The two elders did not recant their wicked tale. Joakim her husband did not come to her rescue astride a white stallion. "A young lad shouted with a LOUD voice, 'I want no part in shedding this woman's blood!" (Dan. 13:46). Maintaining his stance in the midst of the crowd, he chastised them for condemning "the young woman without proper examination and without learning the facts" (Dan. 13:48). The court reconvened and the brilliance of this young man imbued with the spirit of the Lord shone forth. His strategy was one that is used in police interrogations even today—isolate the witnesses and question them separately. They will have no time to fabricate what does not exist.

To elder one, the young man posed the question: "Under what tree did you see them being intimate with each other?" (Dan. 13:54). Elder one's response: "Under the mastic tree."

To elder two, the young man posed this same question: "Under what tree did you catch them being intimate with each other?" (Dan. 13:58). Elder two's response: "Under the evergreen oak."

Caught in their web of lies! Perhaps they never imagined their word would be challenged, so they failed to finalize the details of their vile tale. And now the beauty of the Greek language presents itself in their punishment. Note the linguistic puns.

To elder one's response, "under the mastic tree (*schinos*)" came the punishment: "This lie has cost you your head, for the angel of God has received the sentence from God and will immediately cut (*schinei*) you in two!" (Dan. 13:55).

To elder two's response, "Under the evergreen oak (*prinos*)" came the punishment: "This lie has cost you also your head, for the angel of God is waiting with his sword to split (*prisai*) you in two, so as to destroy you both" (Dan. 13:59). "Acting in accordance with the Law of Moses, they put them to death" (Dan. 13:62).

Who was this young man who succeeded in bringing the conviction of these two vile elders for bearing false witness, breaking the ninth commandment?[92] It was Daniel, the famed prophet who rose to prominence in Babylon. So renowned was his wisdom and reverence of the Lord that even the kings of Babylon respected him. Daniel, his name means "God judges," a name that accords with this story for through him God wrought justice. The story of Susanna clearly holds great significance. It emphasizes virtue, trust in God, the efficacy of prayer and the necessity of proper judicial administration.[93]

But what happened to Susanna? Her father and mother and even her husband Joakim and their relatives "praise God for their daughter Susanna" (Dan. 13:63). "Innocent blood was spared that day"—Susanna's. (Dan. 13:62) But is the beautiful 'lily' of Babylon fully vindicated? Did they always believe her innocent? Were their tears those of the impending judgment and not because she was unjustly accused? On this the text is silent, but I would like to think it did not need to 'speak out.' For just as we the readers know Susanna to be innocent, I would like to see this same belief of innocence more explicitly expressed from her family. Nonetheless, her story has endured through the ages, endearing Susanna, the 'lily' of Babylon, forever in the garden of our hearts.[94]

PART III
Reclaiming...

"Yes, injured Woman! Rise, assert thy right!
Woman! Too long degraded, scorned, opprest..."

—*Anna Laetitia Barbauld*

The Rape of Dinah:
A Quest for Meaning

"*Now Dinah, the daughter of Leah, whom she had borne to Jacob, went out to visit the women of the region. When Shechem son of Hamor the Hivite, prince of the region, saw her, he seized her and lay with her by force. And his soul was drawn to Dinah daughter of Jacob; he loved the girl, and spoke tenderly to her. So Shechem spoke to his father Hamor, saying, 'Get me this girl to be my wife'.*"
(Gen. 34:1-4)

"*He seized her and lay with her by force,*" reads the NRSV translation. The Hebrew literally reads "and he took her and he lay with her and he humbled/afflicted her." The verb rendered 'humbled/afflicted' can be used in the sense of 'mishandling someone' as Sarai did of Hagar (Gen. 16:6), as residents of the Promised Land might do of aliens (Deut. 22:16), or of Job's feelings regarding God's treatment (Job 30:11). But it can also be used, as here, in the sense of a man forcibly having relations with a woman, and as most horrifically exemplified in the story of the rape of the Levite's concubine (Judges 19:24; 20:5).[95]

"*And his soul was drawn to Dinah daughter of Jacob; he loved the girl and spoke tenderly to her.*" The violence that Shechem perpetrated turned to love. The Hebrew more precisely reads "and his soul clung to Dinah daughter of Jacob and he loved the young woman and spoke to the heart of the young woman." "His soul clung," the Hebrew verb /dbq/ "to cling" is most memorably used of Ruth toward her mother-in-law Naomi. Remember how Ruth "clung" to Naomi; she would not part from her regardless of what the future beheld (Ruth 1:14).

"He spoke to the heart of the young woman." The heart is the seat of emotions in Hebraic tradition. "To speak to her heart" is to beseech her very soul, to sway her deepest emotions that his feelings were now those of love not lust. It is a beautiful expression, but one that should send up a warning, for this is the same idiom used of the Levite toward his concubine in Judges 19:3. The Levite ultimately threw out his concubine to be raped to death by the men of the city.

Shechem, his name (like that of his city), means "shoulder," a figurative expression of 'strength, brutality'? His role is active; we hear his voice along with that of his father, Hamor (meaning "ass"). Dinah, her name means "judgment." Her father and brothers will handle her fate; she though central to the story, has no voice. These first four verses of Dinah's story are packed with emotions, key phrases and subtle references. What purpose could this story possibly serve? In what way does Dinah's name behold "judgment?" To answer these questions, consider the development and climax of this story.

In the next scene (Gen. 34:5-17), the setting returns to Jacob's tent and plot of land. Jacob learns that his daughter has been defiled (lit. been made impure), but he holds his peace! He awaits the return of his sons from the field. Shechem's father, Hamor, takes the initiative and comes to speak with Jacob; at the same time the sons of Jacob return from the field. When they learn of Dinah's rape they are enraged. (Consider their response as compared to Jacob's.) Hamor makes his plea, "the heart of my son Shechem longs for your daughter; please give her to him in marriage" (Gen. 34:8). Hamor presents a further resolution, that of intermarriage between Jacob's family and the Shechemites. Then, out of nowhere, Shechem himself appears (Gen. 34:11). Imagine the tension: Hamor and Shechem versus Jacob and ten sons! Shechem pleads for a resolution, "Put the marriage present and gift as high as you like, and I will give whatever you ask me; only give me the girl to be my wife!" (Gen. 34:12). Out of a shocking act of violence comes a resolution that is made in the spirit of correcting the injustice, a resolution now impassioned by love. It is a resolution, moreover, that would restore Dinah's honor.

The sons of Jacob, not Jacob, respond to Shechem's offer; they answered 'deceitfully' (Gen. 34:13). (Take note of this key word.) They cannot give their sister's hand in marriage, nor agree to intermarriage, because the Shechemites are uncircumcised. Circumcision is the sign of the covenant between the Israelites and God (Gen. 17:9-14). The solution is that the Shechemites must be circumcised. In the next scene (Gen. 34:18-24) Hamor and his son Shechem are pleased with this resolution. Shechem "did not delay to do the thing" (Gen. 34:18). They convince the men of the city of Shechem to all be circumcised. And now recall that word 'deceitfully' with which the sons of Jacob had responded to Shechem and his father.

The scene changes (Gen. 34:25-29): three days later while the men of Shechem were in pain, Simeon and Levi, two of Dinah's full brothers "came upon the city unawares, and killed all the males," including Hamor and Shechem (Gen. 34:25-26), "and they took Dinah out of Shechem's house and went away" (Gen. 34:26). Consider amidst the violence done to Dinah, the following negotiations and the circumcisions, Dinah remained in Shechem's home! But the vengeance did not end; the remaining brothers of Dinah came upon the dead and systematically plundered the city: "All their wealth, all their little ones and their wives, all that was in the houses, they captured and made their prey" (Gen. 34:29). The story climaxes in this scene of retribution. Has the violence done to one woman, Dinah, led to retribution against the guilty and the innocent alike?

In the epilogue (Gen. 34:30-31) we learn of Jacob's reaction to his sons actions and their response to Jacob. "Then Jacob said to Simeon and Levi, 'You have brought trouble on **me** by making **me** odious to the inhabitants of the land, the Canaanites and the Perizzites; **my** numbers are few, and if they gather themselves against **me** and attack **me**, **I** shall be destroyed, both **I** and **my** household" (Gen. 34:30).

Jacob is furious with Simeon and Levi out of concern for his status as illustrated by the repetition of 'me, my, I.' Their actions have endangered both he and his household. But what of Dinah's honor? Consider the brothers' response, "Should our sister be treated like a whore?" (Gen. 34:31). Whose response was more appropriate?

Quest for Meaning

On hearing of the act of retribution against Dinah's rape, Jacob thought of himself and his household; Simeon and Levi thoughts were with their sister. The laws of the desert might explain both responses. Jacob and his household lived a semi-nomadic existence, moving from place to place in accordance with the seasons and needs of grazing. When they settled near a town, theirs was a symbiotic relationship with that town, one of give and take. The brothers had violated the unwritten rules of this relationship. When Jacob later blesses his sons in his last Testament (Gen. 49:5-6), he neither forgave nor forgot the actions of Simeon or Levi, "Simeon and Levi are brothers; weapons of violence are their swords. May I never come into their council; may I not be joined to their company—for in anger they killed **me**, and at their whim they hamstrung oxen."

The laws of the desert also dictated that a forceful affront must be matched by an equally forceful act, lest one group lose their respect and authority. The rape of Dinah was the affront, the show of force; it had to be repaid in kind. Whose actions are proper? Jacob's or his sons'? And what of Dinah?

If we look to Rabbinic literature or contemporary scholarship for the answer, we may be disappointed. Rabbinic literature shows its misogynist side. Dinah is called a 'gadabout' who went out dancing and singing with other women hired by Shechem to entice Dinah.[96] According to Josephus, the rape may be her own fault, for she went out to see the finery of the women of Shechem.[97] The renowned biblical commentator, Rashi, provides us with perhaps the most misogynist notion. Dinah's rape was not an offense against her, but against her father. The way to hurt another man is by hurting his women. Jacob deserved this punishment because he had hid Dinah from his brother Esau, fearing that when the brothers reconciled, Esau would demand Dinah's hand in marriage. The violence done to Dinah, from Rashi's perspective, is irrelevant.

Contemporary scholarship in many ways has not done much better. The usual explanation is that since men were responsible for writing down the biblical text, they naturally would disregard the feelings of a woman. But why would this story be preserved in which the men are not presented in a good light? Another response is to negate the rape of Dinah. It did not happen. It is a creation. Ita Sheres proposes this scenario in *Dinah's Rebellion: A Biblical Parable for Our Time.* Dinah and Shechem are star-crossed lovers, like Romeo and Juliet; they come from culturally, religiously, politically opposed societies. Society would not permit them to join in union. Shechem should be the good guy and Jacob and his son the bad guys. The rape story was in effect made up "to poison the readers' impression of a young woman and her prince."[98]

In a contemporary midrash[99] Lauren Deitch, by contrast, acknowledges the 'hurt' done to Dinah, while uniquely retelling this story from Dinah's perspective:

> My name is Dinah. I live in a house full of bickering, noisy people. Nobody listens to me. Nobody understands me. Anyway, one day the yelling was worse than usual and I just walked out the front door. Nobody noticed. I walked a little way and saw a well. Women and girls were gathered about it and they were talking and laughing. I went over there and they talked to me. They seemed genuinely interested in me. It was so pleasant, nobody yelling and arguing. After a while, there were less and less women at the well and I noticed the sun beginning to go down. I didn't know what to do. I didn't want to go back to my house. A young man approached and I felt afraid. But he seemed nice enough and he

was handsome and he spoke softly and politely. He said he was the son of the prince in this region. He said he lived in a big house and it had a wonderful view of the whole city from the roof. He asked if I'd ever been on a really high roof and seen the sun set over the city. So, I walked along with him to his house. It was a huge house, and so tall. I was quite out of breath when we got to the roof. We looked over the edge and the people down there were so small. The sky was all pink and purple. It was so pretty and so very quiet. I told him I'd better go home now. And he said, "Sit awhile." So we sat awhile and talked in the screened roof chamber. Then the bad thing happened and he hurt me and he left. I ran to the door. It was barred from the other side. I cried myself to sleep in the roof chamber.

After a while, I heard a knock and a little maidservant came in with food. She said if she let me out she'd be punished, but I convinced her to run to my house and tell my father to come to get me. So I waited. The little maidservant came and went many times.

On the third day, the screaming started. Not like at my house, but screams of horror, women's screams like I'd never heard before. I looked over the edge of the roof, then backed up quickly. I couldn't look. It was too awful. Then, the door to the roof crashed open and two of my brothers grabbed me and dragged me downstairs and threw me into a cart.

When we got home, everybody was staring at me. Father looked like he was going to explode. I ran to my room. I raised my voice to God, "Why are they mad at me? What did I do?"[100]

The frustration of this young woman born and raised within a patriarchal world is implied in this retelling, as are the innocence, trust and naiveté that would allow her to place herself in such a sexually dangerous position. As compelling as the horror of the 'hurt,' is another 'horror'—she remains in the house while negotiations ensued. Her rescue came amidst another horror, the annihilation of not just the one who caused her 'hurt,' but all those within the city, men and women alike, perhaps the very women and girls she had earlier communed with at the well, perhaps the little maidservant who brought word to her father and sustenance to her. "Why are they mad at me" What did I do?"

writes Deitch of Dinah. Her closing lines reflect the classic guilt transferred from criminal to the victim by society, here her family. In the end Shechem, though dead, is the victor; his fate has been recorded in the biblical text. Dinah, the victim, is forever victimized. Of her fate the biblical text is silent; it is left to later Rabbinic writings (as we will see) to attempt to solicit a mate for this 'impure' maiden.

Barring her brief birth announcement (Gen. 30:21), this story, and her mention in the list of Jacob's offspring who went down to Egypt (Gen. 46:15), Dinah disappears from the biblical text. Rabbinic traditions try to fill this void, relating that Dinah married her brother Simeon because she was dishonored. She went down to Egypt with Jacob and his household and the daughter, Asenath, she conceived from the rape would later marry Joseph. Another tradition relates that Dinah was unmarriageable; she was damaged goods; she remained in Simeon's house as a widow. Dinah has even been named as the second wife of Job, the woman who would bear him ten more children after the tumultuous testing of his faith.[101] These explanations derive from legend or oral tradition; they are not in the biblical text. How then do we put closure to the story of Dinah?

From an anthropological/cultural perspective we might suggest this story demonstrates the laws of the desert. Alternately, Jacob's seeming passivity toward his daughter's rape might by contrast be explained from a biblical perspective. In keeping with biblical law, the 'violation' of a "virgin who is not engaged"—presuming Dinah falls into this category—would result in a fine (fifty shekels) being paid to the father and the young woman would become his wife with the added stipulation that since he violated her he would never be able to divorce her (Deut. 22:28-29). Jacob's actions would appear to follow this Deuteronomic law, with the added caveat, however, that we cannot be certain that this law was yet enacted. The circumcision of Shechem and the men of his town would allow them to join in covenant with God and Israel, and intermarry. The brothers, Simeon and Levi, foiled Jacob's plan with the result that Jacob now returned to the laws of the desert.

If we view this story from a literary perspective we might suggest that this story contributes to the negativity of the city of Shechem in the biblical text. Prior to our story Jacob bought a plot of land from the Shechemites for grazing (Gen. 33:19). In our story we witness the brutality of their prince. Following our story, Jacob buries the idols he gathered from his household beneath an oak near Shechem, a witness to the breaking of covenantal laws within Jacob's own household and his contempt for the city of Shechem (Gen. 35:4). Near the fields of Shechem, Joseph is sold into slavery by his brothers (Gen. 37:14). And finally, when the ten tribes of Israel rebel against Solomon's heir Rehoboam, they set up their new capital, contra Jerusalem, in Shechem (I Kings 12:25). The term Shechem does not evoke pleasant memories.

Perhaps this story might serve as an etiology explaining Dinah's name, a noun derived from the root /dyn/ "to judge," hence "judgement." In Gen. 30, when Leah, Rachel, Bilhah and Zilpah bear 12 sons for Jacob, each is given a name along with an explanation. But for Dinah the text simply states, "Afterwards she [Leah] bore a daughter, and named her Dinah" (Gen. 30:21). Why she is named so we are not told. In what way does she evoke "judgement?" The obvious response is that the Shechemites got their due judgement for Shechem's action. The revenge of Dinah's rape brought proper judgement to the Shechemites and restored the status of Jacob and his family. But this would suggest that Dinah was named in anticipation of being violated.

Another explanation is that Dinah's story is just part of the ongoing events in the Jacob cycle within the Epic of the Patriarchs. Jacob while still in the womb struggled with his twin brother Esau; enmity between brothers continued enmeshed with Jacob's deception. As we read the stories involving Jacob wives, the sisters Rachel and Leah, we find envy and competition. As we read the stories involving his sons we will find impropriety. Reuben, his eldest, sleeps with Jacob's concubine—a sign of contempt and usurpation of authority; Simeon and Levi are involved in the revenge of Dinah; Judah ignores the laws of Levirate marriage and ends up impregnating his daughter-in-law Tamar; Joseph is sold into slavery by his own brothers! Dinah's story would seem to be part of this saga of misfortune and dysfunction that plagued the house of Jacob. It would be a callous statement to say that Dinah is just part of this misfortune; she **is** a victim. What is one of the worst things that could befall a woman? Rape. And rape in the ancient world added the dimension, not present in our western society, of ostracism; she was no longer considered marriageable. Dinah will suffer; the household of Jacob will suffer.

Each biblical story is part of a larger story, yet each story in itself usually presents a lesson. That a lesson is advanced through violence is unfortunate. What is this lesson? Is it an instruction to help us contemplate proper or improper responses in the face of brutality? Jacob's passivity was woefully inadequate, but the brothers' response was in excess. If the law of Deuteronomy (22:28-29) was in existence, Jacob should have given Dinah in marriage. If this law was not yet promulgated, Jacob should have executed only the guilty party, Shechem. Furthermore, in the ancient world Dinah would not have been consulted, no matter how much it bothers our contemporary conscious. Regretfully we cannot apply contemporary standards to events occurring millennia ago. But perhaps we can learn from Dinah's story that violence is non-discriminatory; Jacob's household was a prominent one. Crimes against any individual, especially the helpless, must be punished; however, what degree of retribution is appropriate? Moreover every victim, whether man or woman, deserves to have their voice heard.

Stories like Dinah's are what feminist scholars have labeled *texts of terror*, stories which reflects the brutal abuse of women that can in no way be salvaged as meaningful for contemporary women. Their presence in the biblical text challenges the validity of the entire biblical text for women.[102] Do we abandon Dinah? Erase what is preserved of her because we may not fully understand the import of her story? Hardly! We continue our quest for meaning.

In the end I would like to recall one last legend. It derives Dinah's name not from the Hebrew root /dyn/ judge, hence "judgement," but from the noun /*day*/ "enough, sufficiency." After the birth of twelve sons for Jacob, all the matriarchs exclaimed in joy, "we have **enough** males!" And so Dinah was born. This tale may only be a legend, but it informs us that the generations who created and transmitted this particular legend remembered Dinah, not as the victim of a violent attack, which wrought further dissension on the Jacobian line, but as the beloved daughter finally born into the line of Jacob. The birth of a girl was indeed a cause for celebration!

Tamar: Wife, Harlot, Mother

Our story begins with Judah, fourth son of Jacob and Leah, heading south, away from the fields of Shechem,[103] away from the company of his brothers who had sold their brother Joseph to a caravan of Midianite traders heading towards Egypt. Away, too, he moved from his father Jacob, whom he and his brothers had misled into believing that Joseph had been ravaged by a wild beast. It was *Judah* who had suggested to his brothers that instead of killing Joseph they should make a profit by selling him (Gen. 37:26-27). Perhaps out of remorse Judah leaves the family encampment and heads south where he meets a certain Adullamite named Hirah (Gen. 38:1). He befriends Hirah and settles nearby. The appearance of this friend will serve as a literary device throughout our story signaling a change in events.

Judah marries the daughter of a certain Canaanite whose name was Shua.[104] They have three sons: Er, Onan and Shelah. Judah names the eldest; Shua names their other sons. And then "Judah took a wife for Er his firstborn; her name was Tamar" (Gen. 38:6). Judah's wife is not an Israelite; Tamar's ancestry is unclear, though Rabbinic tradition relates that Tamar was the daughter of Aram, thus related distantly to Abraham.[105]

Our prologue continues with the initial conflict (Gen. 38:6-11): "*Judah took a wife for Er his firstborn; her name was Tamar. But **Er**, Judah's first-born, was wicked in the sight of the Lord, and the Lord put him to **death**. Then Judah said to **Onan**, 'Go in to your brother's wife and perform the duty of a brother-in-law to her; raise up offspring for your brother.' But since Onan knew that the offspring would not be his, he* *spilled his semen on the ground, whenever he went into his brother's wife, so that he would not give offspring to his brother. What he did was displeasing in the sight of the Lord, and he put him to **death** also. Then Judah said to his daughter-in-law Tamar, 'Remain a widow in your father's house until my son **Shelah** grows up'—for he **feared** that he too would die, like his brothers. So Tamar went to live in her father's house."*

"Perform the duty of a brother-in-law" records the text. The custom referred to is that of *yibum*, Levirate marriage. If a man marries a woman and he dies without heir, it is the duty of his closest relative to take her as wife, impregnating her. But the first child born of this union is considered the legal heir of the deceased brother, carrying all the rights and inheritances that would go to the heir of the elder brother. While we may shudder at the ancient custom of *yibum*, we must also consider had Tamar remained a childless widow she would have been relegated to the must vulnerable position in Israelite society. "For nowhere does she belong."[106] While unmarried and a virgin she is under the care and control of her father, once married she is under the care of her husband and his family. Her duty is to produce children. As a childless widow she is not a productive member of her deceased husband's household; she is no longer tied to his clan because it would be through her children that she would maintain kinship ties. She lives in the 'in-between.' The law of the Levir thus protected a young childless widow from social abandonment.[107]

And so Tamar returns to the house of her father, an ineffective, non-productive widow, technically still under the authority of her father-in-law, awaiting Shelah to come of age. Our story continues as conflict turns toward climax.

In the next scene, time has passed. How much time, we do not know, but Judah's wife Shua has died and his time of ritual mourning is complete, literally "he was comforted from her death." He sets out for Timnah to check on his sheepshearers and we encounter his friend Hirah—remember the presence of Hirah is a signal that something is about to happen. Tamar learns that her father-in-law has left, so she removes her widow's garments, puts on a veil, and wraps herself up, in effect disguising her identity. She sits down at the entrance to a city enroute to Timnah, a place called Enaim; in Hebrew it means "eyes." She is upset because Shelah is grown, but had not been given to her.

Judah sees her sitting beside the road; he mistakes her for a *zonah*, a common prostitute, and requests her services, "'Come, let me come in to you,' for he did not know she was his daughter-in-law" (Gen. 38:16). Tamar asks what price he is willing to pay. Judah has not brought along his 'checkbook' or 'cash,' so he offers to send her a kid (goat) later. Service now; pay later.[108] Tamar does not accept this 'later' payment, unless Judah provides a pledge until the kid can be sent (Gen. 38:17). She wants some form of identification that will insure his payment will follow. He asks what would be acceptable and she replies, "Your signet and your cord, and the staff that is in your hand" (Gen. 38:19). The signet and cord refer to a cylinder seal on a cord (a long bead with a hole through which a cord is passed). They are worn around his neck. On the seal we would find a design unique to Judah. When rolled over damp clay, it would be the equivalent of his signature. His walking staff, too, might be personalized through designs. In effect Tamar has asked for the ancient equivalent of his driver's license, state ID card or social security card. Judah agrees, turns over his personal IDs and has relations with Tamar. The text is specific to note, "and she conceived by him" (Gen. 38:18). Tamar returns home, redressing herself in the clothing of widowhood.

We move into a new scene (Gen. 38:20-23). Judah has reached Timnah and his friend Hirah enters the scene. Hirah! We know some new twist in the story is about to unfold. Hirah is sent to recover Judah's pledges, taking in payment the kid. On reaching Enaim he does not "see" her at the city entrance and inquires, "Where is the 'cultic prostitute' *qedeshah* who was at Enaim by the wayside?" (Gen. 38:21). No one has "seen" the *qedeshah*. Note Judah referred to her as a *zonah*, a common prostitute; Hirah inquires after a cultic prostitute, one who would be connected with the rituals of a Canaanite temple. Why the difference? A subtle inference by Hirah that Judah, the Israelite, had participated in a Canaanite religious ritual? When Hirah reports his finding to Judah, Judah replies, "Let her keep the things as her own, otherwise we will be *laughed* at; you see, I sent this kid, and you could not find her" (Gen. 38:23). Remember Judah's response as we enter our third and final scene (Gen. 38:24-26).

We are back in Judah's home, some three months later, but where is Hirah? His absence resounds, for he has signaled each scene along the way. We do not need Hirah to realize that the climax is about to explode! Judah is told, "Your daughter-in-law Tamar has played the whore; moreover she is pregnant as a result of whoredom" (Gen. 38:24). "Played the **whore**," "result of **whoredom**," both terms are derived from the root /znh/, as was the term *zonah* Judah used of Tamar. Judah's response: she is to be brought out and burnt! Burning as a punishment for adultery is attested to in the biblical text; the charge against Tamar would be adultery because she is technically Shelah's betrothed (Lev. 20:10; 21:9).

"As she was being brought out, she sent word to her father-in-law, '"It was the owner of *these* who made me pregnant.' And she said, 'Take note, please, whose these are, the signet and the cord and the staff.' (Gen. 38:25). Tamar's words, "take note, please," are ironically the same words used by Joseph's brothers when they ask Jacob to identify Joseph's torn and bloody robe.

Recreate this scenario in your mind: Tamar, shamed before her family and neighbors, walks downcast OR with head held high toward her execution. Then, while displaying Judah's IDs before all, she sends word to him that the owner of these impregnated her. Of those who beheld Judah's items, how many recognized them? Judah understood to what she referred. Rushing out of his home, he beheld his signet, cord and staff. He "*acknowledged*" them and said, 'She is more in the right than I, since I did not give her to my son Shelah'" (Gen. 38:26). He admitted he had impregnated her and ignored the law of the Levir.

As our story moves into its Epilogue (Gen. 38:27-30) we learn that Tamar is carrying twins, reminiscent of Judah's father Jacob, who was also a twin (Gen. 25:24-26). While Tamar was in labor, the twins struggled, just as Jacob and Esau had. One child put forth his hand. The midwife tied a crimson thread about it just as the hand disappeared back into Tamar's womb. This hand belonged to Zerah, meaning "crimson," technically the first-born. Just then the second child emerged to the exclamation, "What a breach you have made for yourself!" He was named Perez "breach" because, according to Rabbinic tradition, he 'burst forth' from his mother's womb before the older Zerah.[109]

Our story is more than just a case study of the practice of the *yibum*. It is more than just another episode within the Jacob cycle revealing the troubles of his children. Likewise it is more than a story about intermarriage or about how the tribe of Judah settled in the southern region of the Holy Land. For something miraculous comes of this union. If you recall in the essay *Leah of 'Dim' Eyes*, I noted that Leah, though unloved by her husband Jacob, bestowed an eternal gift on Judaism and Christianity, their fourth son Judah. This is the same Judah of our story, through whose lineage we will eventually reach King David and Jesus Christ. Our story is crucial because we learn that it is through Perez, the second born son of Judah and Tamar that the line will extend toward David and Jesus.[110]

What of the relationship between Tamar and Judah? Tamar continued as a widow, for the text is specific to note, "And he [Judah] did not lie with her again" (Gen. 38:26). But Tamar no longer lived on the fringe of society for now she had twins to tie her to a clan. Lest we pass judgement on the actions of Judah or Tamar we might consider this classic line from Rabbinic tradition, "Ye are both innocent! It was the will of God that it shall happen."[111] If you are not quite pleased with this quote, consider this thought. Tamar's name means "palm-tree." A palm-tree bears fruit. Tamar bore the fruit of the Davidic line.

The Levite's Concubine: The Story That Never Was

Introduction

Scholarship traditionally sees the story of the Levite's Concubine in Judges 19-21 and the preceding story of Micah's Shrine (Ch. 17-18) as belonging to a supplement appended to the book of Judges, a supplement whose primary function was to vividly relate the depravity to which Israel had sunk by the end of the period of the Judges, a depravity whose very existence served as the justification for the establishment of kingship in Israel, an institution whose absence is repeatedly brought to our awareness in the refrain "In those days there was no king in Israel"(17:6; 18:1; 19:1; 21:25).

More recently scholarship has redirected its treatment of Judges 19-21, not in challenging this story as belonging to this supplement, but rather in (a) exploring unique elements that illuminate this story and contribute to larger issues;[112] and (b) reconsidering the editorial process as related to Judges 19-21. Yairah Amit's, *The Book of Judges: The Art of Editing*, reconsidered the editorial process of the book of Judges, concluding that while Ch. 19-21 are part of this supplement, they are not of the same nature as Ch. 17-18. Rather she sees Ch. 19-21 as representing the story of a post-exilic author whose intent was to make a political statement: Israel, though dealing with events clearly not ordinary, works as a unity. This unified spirit more properly reflects the earlier period of the Judges (342).[113]

The present paper seeks to draw on the spirit of current redirections—exploring the narrative structure, details and vocabulary of

Judges 19, and evaluating this evidence in light of Amit's post-exilic hypothesis. The inspiration for this study derives from Martin Buber who wrote of the distorted details in this story and its "ahistorical and atypical" nature.[114] Noted comparisons between vocabulary and elements of plot in this story and passages in Genesis, I Samuel and within the book of Judges itself were likewise recognized by Buber, later by Trible (1984) and even earlier by Burney (1918).[115] More recently Bal described the book of Judges as "a book that problematizes languages by proposing uncanny kinds of speech-acts to challenge language as purveyor of meaning."[116] Not only the "problematizing" nature of language in Judges 19 (and 20-21), but the near silence of biblical referents to this tale (one reference to the 'crime of Gibeah' in Hosea 10:9) and the silence of Rabbinic sources and the Church Fathers until the Medieval Period, together create an aura of suspicion and uneasiness that begs for a re-interpretation of this text as a metaphor of dire, not gentle, admonition. These allusions of Israel's past and near future history, pieced together as *tessarae* of a mosaic, present an image of what Israel's destiny *might* become, what women's position *might* become, how brethren *might* become enemies and how this *might* all be (wrongly) accomplished in the name of the Lord.

A Mosaic of Biblical Allusions

The Prologue (Judges 19:1-2) begins with the refrain "in those days there was no king in Israel," a refrain that occurs four times within the supplement to the book of Judges (17:6; 18:1; 19:1; 21:25), twice in the story of Micah and twice in our present narrative. Moreover, in this narrative, the refrain frames the entire story of rape and revenge, being placed strategically at the beginning of the narrative (19:1) and at the very end (21:25). As readers, we are introduced to the two main characters in this prologue: the Levite and his concubine. Neither Levite nor concubine is acknowledged formally by name. Not even Rabbinic legend, so often inclined to provide a name derived from the characters circumstances, has deigned to provide names to our leading characters.[117]

Though unnamed our characters are distinct, created by the contrast of their gender (*'ish/'ishah* "man/woman") followed by a term of status (Levite/concubine).[118] The designation 'Levite' allows us to connect our present story with the preceding one of Micah, who had procured a Levite to initiate at his shrine.[119] Levite as male lead also complacently leads us into a false sense of security. A Levite as a member of the priestly line should be above reproach. Our other protagonist, the concubine, is introduced with the terminology of marriage "and he <u>took</u> for himself a <u>woman</u>," which is then, however, qualified by the noun *pilegesh* concubine. The Levite bears a place of honor in Israelite society; the concubine's place is questionable.[120] Ackerman is well to point out that subsequent references (vv. 4,7,9) indicate she is the Levite's secondary wife.[121] Mention of the word 'concubine' evokes for the reader mixed feelings. It is the concubine Hagar, however, despised, rejected and cast aside who shares the most with the Levite's concubine and who, as we will later see, will subtly be alluded to through action and a familiar idiom.

The residences of our protagonists are also contained within this first verse, providing contrast and allusions. The Levite is from the hill country of Ephraim, the same setting of Micah's home and shrine (Ch. 17), through which the Danite spies and then the Danites marched in their migration and invasion of the northern city of Laish (Ch. 18). The region is recorded as taken by the tribe of Judah in Judges 1:19 and the very same region in which Joshua was buried (Judges 1:9; Joshua 24:30). Looking forward, Elkanah, the father of Israel's last judge, Samuel, was from the hill country of Ephraim (I Sam. 1:1) and the ancient sanctuary of Shiloh where Samuel remained to minister to the Lord was in this same region (I Sam. 2). In the hill country of Ephraim, too, a tall handsome young man would pass through in search of the straying donkeys of his father Kish (I Sam. 9:3-4). To this young handsome man, none other than Saul, we will find other allusions within this story, a young man destined to be the first 'tentative' king, an allusion subtly pushing Israel toward kingship.

By contrast, the concubine is from Bethlehem of Judah, a city that most notably brings to mind the setting of the book of Ruth and begs an allusion to David. Ruth the Moabite would settle in Bethlehem and become the great-grandmother of David who was likewise from Bethlehem (I Sam. 16) and under whom kingship as an institution flourished in Israel. The Levite's home in the hill country of Ephraim distinctly evokes the settings of past biblical stories, while that of the concubine projects us into the future. But it is not only the mention of Bethlehem of Judah that projects us into the future world of Ruth and David for the concubine herself flees back to Bethlehem to her father's house in verse two of our Prologue.

The concubine's flight also brings to mind the flight of another famous concubine, Hagar. Hagar flees not once but twice from the contempt of her mistress, once she returns by command of the angel of the Lord (Gen. 16:9), the second time she does not. The Levite's concubine likewise flees, the cause controversial. Though the Massoretic text states "and his concubine played the harlot against him" (19:2), most translations follow the Greek text's (LXX [A]) reading "and she was angry" suggesting a consonantal confusion of Heh/Het in the final radical of the Hebrew root. The proposed emendation of the MT is reflected by Rabbinic literature which relates that he was harsh and abusive toward her. Josephus likewise records that 'his wife,' did not return his feelings, which in combination with her beauty, aroused his passions even more. Their relationship turned to quarrelling and her departure.

As we move from Prologue to Scene One (Judges 19:3-10) we discover that unlike Abraham who did not go after Hagar, the Levite goes after her "to speak tenderly to her" lit. "to speak upon her heart." Hagar sought refuge in a barren desert, returned safely, fled again to the barren desert and flourished; the concubine sought refuge where one would expect refuge, her father's home and later as a protected guest by the old man of Gibeah, but she did not return safely and was never given an opportunity to flourish. The allusions to Hagar are present, but the irony lies in the distortion of details.

In "speaking to her heart" the Levite is using an idiom that connotes "reassurance, comfort, loyalty, and love."[124] The biblical allusions of this idiom have not gone unnoticed. Trible notes its parallel use in the story of the rape of Dinah, where after raping Dinah, Shechem "loved the young woman and spoke to her heart" Gen. 34:3). The same words are also spoken by Hosea to his wife Gomer" (Hosea 2:14).

Our Levite proceeds on his journey with his servant and a couple of donkeys. The presence of donkeys is a subtle motif used within and beyond this story. Within our story 'the donkeys' appear at critical junctures, indicating a change in scene is about to occur. And so here (v. 3) he sets out on his journey with his donkey. When our Levite reaches his father-in-law's house the text records "the girl's father saw him and came with joy to meet him." The image of a greeting of happy relief brings to mind another story in the book of Judges, in that story, however, it is a young girl who comes out to meet her victorious father, the judge Jephthah, "with timbrels and with dancing" (Judges 11:34). Our image is distorted for it is the father-in-law not the concubine who comes out in welcome. The end result is the same in both stories. Jephthah's daughter will be sacrificed by her father in accordance with his vow to preserve his status and honor (Judges 11:31); the Levite's concubine will be sacrificed by her master to protect himself and his honor. But the concubine's father is not innocent of guilt, for his over-extension of hospitality precipitated the delay that cost the concubine her life. The Levite enjoys the hospitality of his father-in-law's household with the noted repetition of two idioms involving the heart "fortify yourself," (lit. sustain your heart)[19:5,8] and "enjoy yourself" (lit. let your heart be well) [19:6,9]. The heart, to which the Levite wished to speak in v. 3, namely his concubine's, has not been spoken to, rather it is the Levite's heart that has been addressed. Perhaps the only tenderness the concubine has experienced in her father's house is that not once is she called 'concubine.' She is called 'the young woman' in the phrase 'the father of the young woman.' Her status as concubine perhaps is delicately avoided out of respect for her father.

As we move into Scene Two the Levite, after five days, has refused any further hospitality. With saddled donkeys (signaling the scene change) and his concubine (once outside of her father's home we have returned to this epithet), the entourage moves on, but the day is drawing to an end. Jebus, a city of foreigners, is not deemed acceptable, ironic because Jebus is the future city of Jerusalem, taken by David in II Samuel 5. They must move on to the safety of an Israelite city. Their sights are on Gibeah, which belongs to the Benjaminites (19:14,16). The mention of Gibeah and Benjamin leads the reader into a false sense of security. Benjamin, the very name evokes kindly and sympathetic thoughts of past biblical history. It connects us initially with the youngest son of Jacob and Rachel, the son with whom Rachel died in childbirth (Gen. 35:16-20), a son who took no part in the jealousy of his elder brothers against Joseph, a son who was in no way involved in their brother Joseph's sale into slavery, a son whom Jacob—with greatest reservations—sent to Egypt to reclaim Simeon. (Gen. 35,37,42-45). In Moses' final blessing on Israel it is said of Benjamin (Deut. 33:12): "The beloved of the Lord rests in safety—the High God surrounds him all day long—the beloved rests between his shoulders."

We as readers are not prepared for the transformation in character of the Benjaminites in this chapter and in the following two, but perhaps Benjamin's character was hauntingly foretold in Jacob's last words of testament (Gen. 49:27): "Benjamin is a ravenous wolf, in the morning devouring the prey, and at evening dividing the spoil."

The mention of Benjamin takes us most clearly back to Genesis, but moving forward in time the Benjaminites of the Conquest become a vague entity, one tribe among many. The mention of Benjaminites also has one very prominent tie with the institution of kingship. Saul, the first king of Israel was "a man of Benjamin" (I Sam. 9:1-2). The mention of the Benjaminites' city of Gibeah, in our story, likewise, connects us to the future, toward the much-desired institution of kingship, for Gibeah would later become the temporary capital of Saul.

As Scene Three opens (Judges 19:16-21), we find our entourage inside the city of Gibeah, in the open square, without an offer of hospitality. Worries of hospitality are fleeting, as an old man appears who, though presently residing in Gibeah, happens to be from the Levite's region, the hill country of Ephraim. This identification is perhaps to alert the reader that the old man is *not* a Benjaminite, for once again an editorial note reminds us that Gibeah was peopled by Benjaminites (v. 16). The old man questions the Levite in language strikingly similar to Hagar's questioning by the angel; Hagar is asked, "Where have you come from and where are you going?" (Gen. 16:8), the Levite is asked just the reverse "Where are you going and where do you come from?" (Judg. 19:17). The Levite makes mention of his predicament, noting he has fodder for his 'donkeys' and provisions for his *'amah* maidservant (not concubine) and his young man. All he requires is a place to rest. Hospitality is offered with a warning, "do not spend the night in the square." This phrase is hauntingly reminiscent of Lot's warning to the two angelic visitors to Sodom: "Please, my lords, turn aside to your servant's house and spend the night…They said, 'No, we will spend the night in the square.' But he urged them strongly." (Gen. 19:2-3). Lot made them a feast and washed their feet; so too does the old man of Gibeah (vv. 19-21). But the old man also fed the 'donkeys.' If we as readers have not picked up the allusion to Lot's story as a warning against complacency, *the donkeys* at the end of this scene should have signaled a warning.

Our Final Scene (Judges 19:22-28) opens with an idiom of the heart, "they were enjoying themselves" [lit. making their hearts good] (v. 22), immediately sending the reader's thoughts back to the hospitality of the Levite's father-in-law where 'making good' and 'fortifying' their hearts was overflowing. The scene that follows not only disrupts their enjoyment, but also blatantly forces the reader to recall the story of Lot and the Sodomites in Genesis 19. This allusion to the story of Lot and the Sodomites perhaps is the most noted and obvious of all illusions in the story of the Levite's concubine. In Judges 19:22-23 we read:

> "While they were enjoying themselves, the men of the city, a perverse lot, surrounded the house, and started pounding on the door. They said to the old man, the master of the house, 'Bring out the man who came into your house, so that we may know him.' And the man, the master of the house, went out to them, and said to them, 'No, my brothers, do not act so wickedly. Since this man is my guest, do not do this vile thing'."

In Genesis 19:4-7 we similarly find:

> "But before they lay down, the men of the city, the men of Sodom, both young and old, all the people to the last man, surrounded the house; and they called to Lot, 'Where are the men who came to you tonight? Bring them out to us, so that we may know them.' Lot went out of the door to the men, shut the door after him, and said, 'I beg you, my brothers, do not act so wickedly'."

The texts are similar, but not identical. The old man of Gibeah specifically emphasizes the issue of hospitality; one does not harm a guest. It is the host's duty to provide protection. The men of the city are also specifically described as perverse, lit. 'sons of Belial, worthless men.' At Sodom, the literary concern is focused on the inclusiveness of the men, that is from youngest to oldest, an all-encompassing statement. The objective in both cases is to have relations with 'the male guest/guests.' The irony is in our expectation of what will ensue in the Levite's story given the response in the Sodom story.

In Gen. 19:8 Lot offers his two virgin daughters; in Judges 19:24 the host likewise offers two women, his virgin daughter and the Levite's concubine. The host himself offers to bring them out and then adds, 'humiliate/ravish them and do what is good in your eyes to them" (Judg. 19:24). 'Humiliate' or 'ravish,' derived from the Hebrew root *'nh*, is the same verb used of Shechem in Gen. 34:2 when he took Dinah and lay with her and raped her. 'Do what is good in your eyes,' too, is a phrase reminiscent of Lot's words to the men: "do to them as that which is good in your eyes" (Gen. 19:8). It is a phrase that echoes the affliction of another woman, Hagar, of whom Abram said to Sarai, "Behold, your handmaid is in your hand, do to her what is good in your eyes" and "so Sarai humbled/afflicted her,"(Gen. 16:6). Blindness prevented the men of Sodom from any further advances. Our expectations are that similar salvation will prevail for virgin daughter and the Levite's concubine. The virgin daughter of the host is spared, but the Levite himself "seized his concubine and put her out to them" (19:25). The contrast of the expected with reality add to our shocked reaction. The violent abuse follows through the night. When dawn breaks in Lot's story, Lot, his wife and daughters are led out of the city to safety; when dawn breaks for the Levite's concubine she is released and returns to the host's house, only to collapse.

This scene concludes with perhaps the most disturbing action, reaction and words in the entire narrative:

> "In the morning her master got up, opened the doors of the house, and when he went out to go on his way, there was his concubine lying at the door of the house, with her hands on the threshold. 'Get up,' he said to her, 'we are going.' But there was no answer." (Judg. 19:27-28)

Indifference is the response of the Levite to the lifeless form of his concubine, her hands in a death-grip on the threshold of the door. This is the door through which she had earlier walked for refuge and out of which she had been thrown. His response is unconscionable. But the horror of indifference is magnified many times if the reader is careful to notice the biblical allusions in his truncated two curt words "arise (*qum*) and let us go (*bo'*)" with that of the rustic lover in the Song of Songs "arise (*qum*) my beloved, my fair one, and come (*bo'*)"

(2:10,13). Our passage leaves out those tender words "my beloved, my fair one,' words the text initially implied when the Levite went after his concubine "to speak tenderly to her" (Judg. 19:3). Bereft of words of tenderness, all that remain are commands that pay no heed to the abuse she has suffered. She does not respond. The Greek text specifically states she is dead; the Hebrew alludes to it with "and there was no answer." His words "get up and let us go," however, are not words that call for response but for action.

As this final scene closes HE fulfills the action. Our donkey once again appears to carry her lifeless body home. A striking irony presents itself with the last appearance of the donkey that carries the abused and dead body of the concubine on her return trip home. It is an image that so hauntingly brings to mind the image of another young woman in Chapter 1 of the book of Judges, Achsah, who rode alone by donkey from her home in the Negeb to her father's home in Hebron to procure springs of water for her household. Achsah's is an image of a woman riding into a future bright with possibilities; the lifeless body of the Levite's concubine draped over the donkey has no future, save dismemberment that leads to further atrocities.[125]

The Resolution of our story is found in Judges 19:29-30. The Levite returned home and "he took the knife," just as "Abraham took the knife" in Genesis 22:10 to offer Isaac as a sacrifice at the Lord's request. The angel stayed the hand of Abraham; no one stays the Levite's hand. And the Levite, "grasping his concubine cut her into twelve pieces, limb by limb" (Judg. 19:29). The Levite distributes (*nth*) these pieces amongst the tribes of Israel just as Saul had cut up an oxen and distributed the pieces (*nth*) throughout Israel as a call to war (I Sam 11:7). The message is clear. The Levite has suffered an affront. What will Israel do about it? His concubine, his possession, has been damaged. Retribution must be wrought. He asks Israel to "consider it, take counsel and speak out" (Judg. 19:30). The expression 'consider it' in Hebrew is literally "to place the heart" *sim leb*; however, in our verse the idiom has been truncated *simu*—the word 'heart' *leb* has been omitted. The Levite has most subtly omitted his heart, his compassion, his love for his concubine.

A mosaic of allusions exists not only in Judges 19, but continues in Judges 20-21 when Israel responds to the Levite's cry for vengeance. Most noteworthy are allusions to the cities of Mizpah, Jabesh-gilead, and the Lord's support during battles of conquest. The manipulation of these cities and the way in which the Lord demonstrates support during battle once again connects the ensuing chapters of vengeance with past events in Genesis, Joshua and Judges, and future events in I Samuel.

The Story That Never Was

Reading this story as metaphor of admonition, as 'atypical and ahistorical', concurs with Amit's suggestion that the events in Judges 19 and the retribution, which follows in Ch. 20-21, are not 'ordinary'. Seeing this story as a post-exilic composition appended to the book of Judges if not to the supplement in Judges 17-18 likewise concurs with Amit's editorial research. Where this analysis parts with Amit's is in locating the chronological referent to our story. Amit, as earlier noted, sees Judges 19-21 as reflecting the period of the Judges itself, based on the political unity demonstrated in tribal response to the demise of the Levite. The present analysis of language and narrative style in Judges 19 alone suggests the opposite, favoring the traditional understanding of Judges 19-21 as representative of the utter depravation at the end of the period of the Judges. The distortion of biblical passages in Judges 19 represents the hypothetical apex of woman's oppression that could be wrought. If the story horrifies us, it is because it was designed to do so. If its distorted allusions to other biblical phrases and events upset our expectations, then they have achieved their purpose. They have weighted our souls with a sense of foreboding that all is not well. They have surreptitiously informed us that all was not right with the world of Israel at the end of the period of the Judges. The acts of retribution that ensue likewise reflect society in all its manifestations needed to be reordered. 'Mob rule' is not the equivalent of a unified political organization that solves the problems, as Amit suggests.

Read as a metaphor of admonition, however, the tale of the Levite's Concubine delivers a much more powerful message. Israel has gone astray, far more than in the earlier period of the Judges when a charismatic leader imbued with the spirit of the Lord could deliver Israel from its external oppression and bring her back to God. But a judge was not enough, even if the spirit of the Lord descended upon him or her, because the enemy that oppressed Israel was not Cushan-risathaim of Aram-naharaim, not the Moabites, not the forces of Sisera or the Amalekites, not the Midianites or the Philistines. The enemy was from within, Israel herself; she was her own oppressor.

A dynamic, horrific tale was crafted to save Israel this time, not a judge, and so 'the story that never was' was created, fashioned by the distortion of the very phrases and details of a text held so sacred. The allusions may have been quite apparent to those centuries closer to the text's formation; they would have seen through the literary veil and understood the moral of this tale. Millennia later we too can see through this veil and reclaim this story, viewing it not as a historical text of terror, but a horrific and effective metaphor of warning…for such a thing has *never* happened since the day that the Israelites came up from the land of Egypt until this day!…but it could!

◆　　◆　　◆

In the Spring of 2002, while preparing for a special topics course on the Legacy of the Hebrew Bible, I chanced upon a slim volume that contained reproductions of the etchings of Rembrandt.[126] The objective of this course was to not only inform the student of the contents, nature, and growth of the Hebrew Bible, but just as importantly to acquaint them with the influence of this text on such disciplines as art, music and literature. This volume would indeed complement other resources gathered for discussions of the Hebrew Bible's influence on art.

The etchings of Rembrandt contained in this collection were inspired by both the stories of the Hebrew Bible and the New Testament, with depictions of the expected—the Creation, The Fall, the parting of the Red (Reed) Sea, Christ carrying the Cross and more. Expected turned to surprise at etching number 16: *A Man of Gibeah Offers Hospitality to the Levite and His Concubine* (1645). The subject matter of the Levite's Concubine—as the paper I had currently been researching revealed—was scarcely taken up by artists through the centuries.[127]

Rembrandt's etching presented the old man of Gibeah just as the old man meets the Levite in the open square of Gibeah. The composition is arranged is such a fashion so that the two men stand to the right of center, ostensibly discussing an offer of hospitality. To the left we find the donkey, in front of which sits the clearly exhausted concubine, seated upon of log beside a well. Her chin rests upon her left hand, elbow resting upon the edge of the well. Her right hand lays limp at her side, loosely holding the hat that once shielded her head from the sun's heat. It was not the visible signs of her exhaustion that caused me to take an astonished second look, nor the posturing of the Levite and old man, nor the presence of the donkey, nor the very sketchy outline of another donkey and servant in the left background. Beside the concubine's hat, from behind the log, peers a child—perhaps a little over a year old. The child's head, right shoulder and arms are all that is visible. His posturing suggests he (?) is trying to pull himself upon the same log whereon is seated the concubine, his mother (?). The disinterest of the concubine toward the child almost suggests the child does not exist. There is no child in the biblical narrative, or mention in rabbinic sources. Whatever inspired Rembrandt remains a mystery; however, his subtle addition sparks the potential for further speculation. We might consider this etching of a child, light in tone, slight in detail—rivaled only in incompleteness by the background rough draft of donkey and servant—as delivering a most powerful message. Rembrandt's 'child' reminds us that a child may have figured in this story, both literally and figuratively. The Levite's concubine may have a child, preserving her own lineage and that of the Levite, or the sketchiness of the child's depiction and the indifference of the concubine may have been added to suggest the future potential of a child for this couple. At this point in the narrative the Levite has retrieved his concubine; they have a future together that could include children, a future, however, that never came to fruition.

Rembrandt's 'child' compels us to entertain the metaphorical in the image of this small child. Israel, as earlier suggested, is the Levite's concubine, oppressed, abused, raped and murdered. Her oppressors are none other than Israel herself. In the square of Gibeah, however, Israel still had the potential to rebuild herself, to bring forth innocence and purity, to bring forth a new Israel. In the town's square in Gibeah, forebodings were present, but the potential, too, as envisioned by Rembrandt, presented in the form of a small child, was present. When the Levite threw his concubine out to the men of Gibeah, her passage beyond the sanctum of the old man's house, over the threshold of his door, marked the collapse of this potential. What more touching symbol for potential and horrific symbol for potential lost than in the intimation of hope aroused by the almost hidden figure of a very young child. Such speculation may have been left unconsidered had not the pen of Rembrandt perhaps subconsciously added a most profound detail.

Overture:
She Walks in Beauty

She Walks in Beauty Like the Night: Proverb's Woman of Valor

SHE walks in beauty, like the night
Of cloudless climes and starry skies;
And all that's best of dark and bright
Meet in her aspect and her eyes...
                            —Lord Byron

Tradition records that Lord Byron wrote these exquisite words inspired by the breathtaking beauty of Mrs. Wilmot, his cousin by marriage. Every head turned in awe as she graced the society ball in a gown of deepest black with sparkles aglitter. Beauty, however, is more than comely countenance and fine carriage:

...her face;
Where thoughts serenely sweet express
How pure, how dear, their dwelling-place.

...The smiles that win, the tints that glow,
But tell of days in goodness spent,
A mind at peace with all below,
A heart whose love is innocent!

The beauty, the charm, the grace of Lord Byron's Mrs. Wilmot, the radiance and softness of her aura, come from "days in goodness spent" and serenity from "a mind at peace." Byron's *belle lettre* has become immortalized as a description that bespeaks the ideal woman.

I have heard it said that once a literary creation is released to the world it takes on a life of its own. And so I take the liberty, my esteemed readers, of considering Lord Byron's words as I consider the Bible's vision of the ideal woman, *'eshet hayil*, the woman of valor, in Proverbs 31:10-31.

◆ ◆ ◆

"A capable wife who can find?
She is far more precious than jewels.
(Prov. 31:10)

"A capable wife" is the NRSV's translation of Hebrew *'eshet hayil*. But *'eshet* simply means "woman," becoming wife by context. *Hayil* means "strength, valor, ability; wealth; even force, i.e. an army." "Capable" does not do justice to the Hebrew or the sentiments that follow. The rhetorical question, with which our proverb begins, *'eshet hayil mi yimtsa'* "a woman of valor, who can find?" expects the response, "No one!" But then paradoxically the rest of this proverb presumes such a woman exists. Her value is incomparable; her valor is not achieved with ease.

How was this 'woman of valor' perceived some two to three thousand years ago when our proverb was composed? She was a woman prized and praised for her domestic duties. But consider the range of these duties. She was up before dawn to prepare for the needs of her family, yet "Her lamp did not go out at night,"(Prov. 31:18), still burning steadily with these duties. She was valued for the trust her husband placed in her that his needs and that of their household would be attended to. Her children, too, praise her for her direction and wisdom. Her attentiveness reached beyond the home to the poor and the needy. While her husband is known at the city gates—a place for congregating and transacting business—she, too, is praised at the city gates for her work! She is industrious, resourceful, a selfless wife and mother; she is altruistic. She performs household duties, but she is also a home manager, a teacher to her children, a shrewd bargainer in the market place, a manufacturer of fine garments, one responsible for business transactions and an advocate for the needy. But above all she reveres the Lord (Prov. 31:30). I have no doubt that the biblical *'eshet hayil* is reflected in Lord Byron's verse: *The smiles that win, the tints that glow,*

But tell of days in goodness spent. Just as the goodness of Mrs. Wilmot exceeded the sparkle of her gown, so too is Proverb's *'eshet hayil* "far more precious than jewels" (Prov. 31:10).

Some of the sentiments and details of this proverb may seem timebound, a reflection of ages gone by, reflecting the ideal woman from what has often been deemed a man's perspective—a housewife. Indeed feminist scholarship has seen this proverb as discriminatory, reinforcing the old adage "a woman's place is in the home." As a graduate student I recall a certain Jewish professor relating that his wife refused to recite this proverb at the opening of their Sabbath home service because to her it had always evoked feelings of women's subjugation. I recall, too, the repercussions from another occasion, during my early years of teaching Biblical Hebrew, when a student told me he had written this proverb in a letter to his beloved. She was not pleased; she interpreted it as a harbinger of the type of wife he expected her to be. To view this proverb as teaching that women are destined and good for only one purpose—domesticity—misses its timeless message and ignores the significance of its details. Byron's Mrs. Wilmot "walked in beauty" because of her good deeds, so too does our *'eshet hayil*. The nature of these good deeds in one respect is irrelevant; a woman who gives of the best of her abilities to her husband, children, family, community *and/or* chosen career AND who reveres the Lord is to be praised.

The woman of Proverbs 31:10-31 is not the only biblical *'eshet hayil*. Later Rabbinic tradition preserves a list of twenty-two women who achieved the status of an *'eshet hayil*:

> Noah's wife, Sarah, Rebekah, Leah, Rachel, Bithiah (Moses' fostermother), Jochebed, Miriam, Hannah, Jael, the widow of Zarephath, Naomi, Rahab, Bath-sheba, Michal, Hazlelponith (Samson's mother), Elisheba (Aaron's wife), Serah (Asher's daughter), wife of the prophet Obadiah, the Shunammite, Ruth and Esther.[128]

Many of these names are familiar; others may elicit a vague recollection, while others still may bring a total blank to our minds.[129] Each one is deemed an *'eshet hayil* not in recompense for their domestic skills, but rather because:

- She gives birth to a son who will be crucial to the future of Israel, often after barrenness and divine intervention.

- She performs a selfless act to care for a 'man' (son, husband, brother, prophet) who will be or is crucial to Israel.

- She is a heroine, in some way saving her people from their enemies.

Of the women we have re-imagined, remembered and sought to reclaim—Eve, Lilith, Sarah, Lot's Daughters, Leah, Micah's mother, Mrs. Job, Vashti, Susanna, Dinah, Tamar and the Levite's Concubine—only Sarah and Leah have made the 'Rabbinic' list. That Lilith, Lot's daughters or Micah's mother were excluded is of no surprise. But what of the others; that they did or were a part of or served some extraordinary purpose is obvious. That they diverge from Proverbs' profile of an *'eshet hayil* is likewise obvious. However, the Rabbinic definition of *'eshet hayil* also diverged.

Proverbs' *'eshet hayil* like Lord Byron's Mrs. Wilmot narrowly defines the quintessential goodness and beauty, external and internal, of a specific type of woman. The Rabbinic 'list' refined this notion to emphasize valor through giving birth to, caring for a significant male character or saving one's people. In the preceding essays (and papers) this notion is extended further, valor may still embrace the Proverbial and Rabbinic notions, but the possibilities are endless. The re-imagining of Eve asked the reader to revisit the role of Eve in relation to Adam and view her, nay their, world as paradigmatic of the first human relationship from a biblical perspective, a relationship of 'beloved and friends' (as playwright and lyricist Elizabeth Swados projects), yet filled with the reality of a true relationship—for better or worse, in good times or bad, in sickness and in health, till death do us part. Perhaps by this re-imagining centuries of negativity can be erased and we envision their world through the immortal words of Robert Browning "Grow old with me/the best is yet to be." Sarah's and Leah's remembrance clearly accords with the Rabbinic value of an *'eshet hayil*, while remembering, Mrs. Job, Vashti and Susanna challenged us to find the valor that has been overlooked or forgotten for each woman. Perhaps the words of Christina Rossetti (1830-94) that preface this section can now hold greater import:

> Remember me when I am gone away...
> Yet if you should forget me for a while
> And afterwards remember, do not grieve...
> Better by far you should forget and smile,
> Than that you should remember and be sad.

Rosetti's words echo her fear of being forgotten by the man whom she loved. She asks to be remembered, but acknowledges that one may very well 'forget me for a while.' More importantly the remembrance that follows forgetfulness should not be grief-stricken. We may wish to grieve or be sad when we consider in particular the fate of Mrs. Job, Vashti or even the tribulation of Susanna. But rather than 'forget and smile' as Rossetti writes, we should remember and appreciate the value and valor of each woman.

When we try to reclaim—as with Dinah, Tamar and the Levite's Concubine—we must acknowledge the pain and injury of these women, as Anna Laetitia Barbauld (1743-1825) did of womankind in her poem "The Rights of Woman": Yes, injured Woman! Rise, assert they right!/Woman! Too long degraded, scorned, oppress. Acknowledgement, however, is not enough and so we sought the reason for the preservation of their stories in the biblical text. In this way we can reclaim these texts for contemporary society, acknowledging their pain and oppression, while understanding that their oppression delineated the flaws and struggles of biblical society: Dinah, demonstrating the struggle between the laws of the desert and brotherly desire for vengeance; Tamar, revealing justice may need be achieved while breaking the accepted conventions; and the Levite's concubine, perhaps the most horrendous tale of oppression asks us to take the greatest leap to achieve reclamation—denying the literal truth of a story and positing the presence of metaphor as a aphoristic tool.

But what of re-imagining Lilith, Lot's Daughters or remembering Micah's mother. My proclivities are not to re-imagine Lilith as the first feminist nor fondly remember Micah's mother because both depict the antithesis of what a woman, a wife, a mother should be. Lot's daughters, perhaps, should be left in the world of etiologies. Realism, however, present both in legend and the biblical text does and should exist. Lilith and Micah's mother, among such others as Jezebel, to some Delilah, reveal another side of human nature: not every woman is an *'eshet hayil*. Our acquaintance with such women is just as valuable. Not all can 'walk in beauty like the night.' And so the value of re-imagining, remembering and reclaiming is in recognizing this truth; each woman with whom we have but briefly shared these pages has a role and a purpose. If the thoughts and speculations presented within these pages has led the reader to stop and challenge past preconceptions, be 'astonied' or inquisitive at the unexpected, then neither these women nor my words have been in vain.

Reimagining, remembering and reclaiming through the lenses of such diverse media and disciplines as music, lyrics, literature, poetry, and art have allowed us to reconsider in the preceding pages a legacy lost, hidden or overshadowed through centuries of literary, textual, religious, spiritual and societal abuse of the biblical text. Such reconsidering can enrich the text, validate personal proclivities, expand the potential embedded in the story of each woman—and in truth need not be limited to a cast of the female gender. The journey begun here is just a beginning; my speculations are not the only valid ones or finite in respect to a story or character. The potential is limited only in so far as we wish to limit our energies or willingness to search, to experience, realizing that at any time on the road of life may appear some blatant or subtle sensory experience that can add to or alter our conceptions of the biblical characters that have been so influential to western humanity.

◆ ◆ ◆

On the big island of Hawaii, on the leeward side, the Kona Coast, about twenty miles south of the quaint, historically laden town of Kailua-Kona, we came upon the "Painted Church." I had read about this church in my Frommer's Guidebook, a 'must-see,' a valuable site that figured prominently in the missionary history of the Hawaiian Islands. Located in the hills just above the sacred ancient site of Pu'uhonua O Honaunau "the place of refuge" for Hawaiians who had broken a *kapu*, we nearly missed the site's entrance to our left—in fact the first time through we did—as our eyes focused on the King Kamehameha road sign on the right. (Kamehameha markers were used throughout the island to point out sites of significance.) The entrance was marked with two signs: on the right stood the more recent St. Benedict's Catholic Church, on the left the original weather-worn St. Benedict's, the Painted Church, established 1900 by Father John Berchmans Velghe. At the top of a short winding road stood a contemporary community building, to the left the quaint white-washed St. Benedict's Painted Church. Ascending the stairs demands a pause at the top for a look back at the breath-taking view of Ho'okena Bay and beyond to the Pacific Ocean. A glimpse within validates the epithet, *the Painted Church*, "a page from Michelangelo" (309) as Frommer's Guidebook noted.

On entering the church my attention was drawn to the altar flanked by a statue of the Madonna to the right and Jesus to the left, both adorned with leis. The altar cloth, too, bore the marks of the Hawaiian culture—a straw-colored tapu cloth, with earthy-brown markings, such as the kona turtle of ancient Hawaii—clearly the synthesis of

Hawaiian and Christian tradition were visible within this tiny church. Likewise this synthesis was present on the white and red-striped columns bearing biblical inscriptions in the Hawaiian tongue—the only word I could discern was SATANA. Upwards the columns burst into palm fronds, set against a ceiling painted to suggest complex barrel vaulting highlighted with stars. Again the contrast belies Hawaiian and European traditions. My eyes were then drawn to the church walls; here the inclination to draw comparison to Michelangelo's Sistine Chapel became evident.

Interior of St. Benedicts's Painted Church

On entry to the Sistine Chapel, Michelangelo, employing the medium of frescoe, painted a series of panels on the arched vault. The focus of these frescoes chronologically proceeded in reverse from the drunkenness of Noah after the Flood to Creation. The Old Testament world on the ceiling met the New Testament world on the wall behind the altar where the Last Judgment is richly detailed. The side registers likewise depict biblical prophets and sibyls. The Sistine Chapel served as visual testament to the legacy of beauty, splendor, glory, sin and judgment as revealed in the biblical text.

Back in Honaunau, Hawaii, Fr. Velghe likewise wished to leave a visual testament, his medium, however, was the modest house paint. Three registers adorned each side of the church: on entering, to the left was first Belshazzar's Feast from the Book of Daniel with "the writing on wall" painted on this wall; next the Temptation of Christ at the moment when Christ stands victorious on the precipice and Satan is flung into the Judean abyss; lastly a Benedictine friar, hands raised waist-high in exultation at the vision of the Christ upon the cross transposed against the wings of a dove. The right wall (on entering) likewise preserved three registers: a vision of Hell; a woman in the peaceful repose at death with assurance of salvation intimated by the light aglow from an open door at the background left; and finally Cain, Abel and Eve, with Eve trying to resuscitate Abel! The desire to discover the significance of Velghe's arrangement of paintings was tucked into the recesses of my mind in favor of musing over the inspiration for this final painting. I did not recall such an event within the biblical narrative (Gen. 4). Had he been influenced by European painters, like Fra. Bartolommeo's *The Creation of Eve* which sought to present a more positive biblical text for the Renaissance world? Did Father Velghe, too, wish to impart a more 'positive' or more human portrait of the biblical cast to his Hawaiian audience? At the turn of the century had he stood at the pulpit and delivered a sermon on the motherly reaction of Eve, punctuating the heart-wrenching human emotion of a mother's loss with one hand extended toward this visual? Though the ancient Hawaiian religion was clearly not pacificistic, his ability to retain those who had converted to Christianity, as well as gain new believers, may have depended on how he presented the biblical stories.

Painting was a visual way of teaching for Father Velghe, as evidenced not only by the Painted Church. He had also painted the walls of his former parishes throughout Polynesia, the Church of Maria Lanakila (also on the Big Island), and continued to paint (and teach) on returning to his native Belgium in 1904. In Belgium he likewise trained a young Belgian student, the future Father Evarist, to paint. Father Evarist would later be sent to Hawaii where he also painted two churches on the Big Island.[130]

The unique theology of Father Velghe's painting of the *Resuscitation of Abel* had instantaneously caught my attention, pleading with me to reconsider, to re-imagine, again, Eve. The message of Father Velghe preserved in the legacy of this painting may have been so commonplace for the Hawaiian parishioners of St. Benedict's, but had its impact been lost with time? I had entertained a similar notion in my re-imagining of Eve and Adam, but not to this extent. The music and lyrics of Elizabeth Swados, and Fra. Bartolommeo's *The Creation of Eve* had helped abolish—at least in my mind—the preconceptions perpetuated by Milton and Christian theology that Eve need only be thought of as the source of original sin. But after joining Eve with Adam as 'beloveds and friends' this unexpected discovery pleaded with me to consider that, though part of a relationship, Eve (and Adam) could also individually carry a message.

Eve, 'Havvah,' is the mother of all the living states the biblical text (Gen.3:20), a name bestowed by Adam; however, what of Eve as simply the mother of her first sons, the twins, Cain and Abel. The text does not belie the nature of their relationship; it just leaves the details unstated. But Father Velghe had the foresight to envision Eve, the mother, arched over the fallen body of Abel, cupping his head between her hands. Gently she lifts his head towards her, as if to breathe into him the very life she one gave to him. Her posture, her facial expression, her garb reflect the trauma, the anguish of a most unconscionable deed. Slightly to the background, near the head of both Abel and Eve, stands the culprit Cain, but his visage is not one of pride. His face has dropped into his left hand, covering but half of his face, that which is exposed reveals the disbelief of his action. His other hand, hanging

144   Re-Imagining Eve and Adam

limply to the front of his body, loosely grasps the club, his weapon of revenge; the stance of his body suggests the very club that took Abel's life now supports Cain. The tones and hues employed by Velghe are dark and somber; the water-damage adds to the serious nature of the scene.

Resuscitation of Abel

Theologians, scholars and lay people alike have been inclined to focus on the story of Cain and Abel as depicting the first murder, analyzing the reasons for Cain's actions, analyzing the virtue of one son over the other. Father Velghe's painting suggests another message in this story, perhaps a message as simple as one's actions reach beyond the immediate, rippling onward and outward. Cain's actions harmed Abel and Eve, and from here the repercussions no doubt were felt by Adam and everyone on hearing this tale. For the present writer the chance discovery of Velge's *Resuscitation of Abel* at this particular moment in time, added to an unexpected acquaintance with Fra. Bartolommeo's *The Creation of Eve* (as noted in the lead essay), combined with my chance introduction to Rembrandt's *The Levite's Concubine* (closing essay), reminded me that the re-imaginings, the rememberings, the reclaimings contained within these pages, contemplated and composed over the past six years, are not final thoughts, not the overture, but the prelude to potential interpretations that await discovery often through the unexpected not ordinarily considered in the pursuit of biblical wisdom.

Endnotes

1. Anthony Newley and Leslie Bricusse, "Pure Imagination." Arranged by Kenny Loggins, David Benoit and David Pack. *Kenny Loggins: Return to Pooh Corner.* Sony Music Entertainment, 1994.

2. *The Atlantic Monthly.* 282.3 (1998): 114-116.

3. The essays contained in this collection are revisions based on and inspired by the two adult education series *Bible Women: Ancient Images and New Perspectives* and *Remembering Those Forgotten,* originally developed for and delivered at Congregation Emanuel B'ne Jeshurun (Milwaukee, WI 1996). These series in full or in part were likewise delivered at various other congregations, centers and institutions in Wisconsin, Arizona, and Washington. A number of these essays were also published online at Themestream.com.

4. *"Do Not Reject Your Mother's Teaching?!": The Role of Micah's Mother in Judges 17* was delivered at the Midwest Regional Joint Conference of the Society of Biblical Literature and the American Academy of Religion (Marquette University, Milwaukee, WI, 1996). *About Sarah* is a revision of a seven part series originally published by Themestream.com (2000-01). *"The Levite's Concubine: The Story That Never Was,"* accepted for presentation at the Pacific Northwest Regional Joint Conference of the SBL and AAR (University of Oregon, Eugene, OR, 2002), though not presented due to unfortunate circumstances, was presented to the Jewish Student Organization at Central Washington University (Ellensburg, WA, 2002).

5. Blaise Pascal, The Provincial Letters Pensées Scientific Treatises. William Benton Publisher, 1952: Lettres provincialis XVI.

6. Milan Entertainment, 1995. Swados' musical journey through biblical history uses the vehicle of contemporary song to relate the adventures, the triumphs, the tragedies of a few prominent, but representative biblical women, women whose stories and historical settings may be distinct, but whose responses and reactions are universal. Her journey defies historical order, moving from Persian times (Vashti and Esther) to the time of the Judges (Ruth), back to the period of the Exodus (Miriam), back to Patriarchal times (Sarah) into Primeval times (Lilith and Eve), and closing with a giant leap forward once again to the time of the Judges (Deborah). The musical is framed by an opening adaptation of Proverbs 31:10-31 "A Woman of Valor," closing with a triumphal and inspirational finale "Sing Unto the Lord a New Song." Each woman highlighted is accredited as a woman of valor, triumphal in her setting and timelessly inspirational.

7. L. Ginzberg, *The Legends of the Jews*. JPS, 1925; Vol. I (1909):74; Vol. IV (1925): 95.

8. *The Norton Anthology of World Masterpieces*. 7th ed. Vol. 1. W.W. Norton & Company, 1999: 2245.

9. Josephus, *Antiquities of the Jews*, 2.52, notes of Adam and Eve, "They also had daughter;" and 2.68 "He had indeed many other children, but Seth in particular.' (In *The Works of Josephus: Complete and Unabridged*. Updated Edition. Translated by William Whiston, A.M. Hendrickson Publishers, 1987.) See also Ginzberg (V:135) where haggadic legend recalls that Cain, Abel and their twin-sisters were born on the day Adam and Eve were created.

10. *Antiquities of the Jews* I.48 "However, Adam excused his sin, and entreated God not to be angry at him, and laid the blame of

what was done upon his wife; and said that he was deceived by her." (In *The Works of Josephus: Complete and Unabridged*. Updated Edition. Translated by William Whiston, A.M. Hendrickson Publishers, 1987.)

11. All excerpts of Milton's *Paradise Lost* are from *The Norton Anthology of World Masterpieces: The Western Tradition*. 7th ed. Vol. 1. New York: W.W. Norton & Company, 1999: 2197-2256.

12. *Questions and Answers on Genesis* I,46. In *The Works of Philo: Complete and Unabridged*. New Updated Version. Translated by C.D. Yonge. Hendrickson Publishers, 1993.

13. See P. Jouon, S.J. *A Grammar of Biblical Hebrew*. Vol. I. Translated & Revised by T. Muraoka. Roma, 1996:61-69.

14. Little, Brown and Company, 1996: 32-33.

15. *Bible Women: Ancient Images and New Perspectives* was an adult education course developed by Dr. Szpek in conjunction with Elizabeth Swados' *Bible Women* (see Re-Imagining Adam and Eve). This course was taught by Dr. Szpek at Congregation Emmanuel B'ne Jeshurun in Milwaukee, WI (1996-1997) and at the Jewish Community Center in Tucson, AZ (1998).

16. See p. 21

17. See pp. 21-22.

18. See. p. 23.

19. See. p. 23.

20. On Lilith in Ancient Mesopotamia see, for example, the discussions of Robert Graves and Raphael Patai, *Hebrew Myths: The Book of Genesis*. New York: McGraw-Hill Book Company, 1964; Samuel Noah Kramer, The Sumerians: *Their History, Culture and Character*. University of Chicago Press, 1963.

21. Louis Ginzberg, *The Legends of the Jews*. JPS. Vol. I (1909): 65-66; Vol. V: 40.

22. See F. Brown, S.R. Driver & Ch. Briggs, *A Hebrew and English Lexicon of the Old Testament*. Oxford: Clarendon Press, 1951: 539.

23. The deuterocanonical text, The Wisdom of Ben Sira (aka Ecclesiasticus), is found in the Apocrypha, a collection of text deemed authoritative by the Catholic Church, but outside the canonical collection in Judaic and Protestant circles. It dates to the 2nd BC and is concerned with religious truth with special emphasis on worldly wisdom that comes from experience as reported by the scribe Jesus ben Sira renowned for his wisdom.

24. So, for example, He [The Teacher] said to him [Ben Sira], "Say [a proverb beginning with the letter] Lamedh." He responded, "Don't [lo'] act old during your youth; in your old age don't take an old woman, because an old woman will weaken your strength, but a virgin adds to your strength and might."…He [The Teacher] said to him, "Say [a proverb beginning with the letter] Mem." He responded, "the waters [memey] of a virgin are sweet and add strength, but the waters of an old woman are as bitter as wormwood and drain strength like a pit in which there is water, but water drawn away by the wind."

25. The Ineffable Name of God refers to the Tetragrammaton, the four letters YHWH, which traditionally represent the Lord's proper name. Due to the sacredness of His name it should not be pronounced, rather the reverent Adonai 'My Lord' should be pronounced whenever the name appeared in the text, other literature and even prayers. For the treatment of the tetragrammaton in pointed (vocalized) texts, see J. Weingreen, *A Practical Grammar for Classical Hebrew*. 2nd ed. Oxford: Clarendon Press, 1959: 23.

26. See Ginzberg, V: 148.

27. The term Shekinah "divine presence" developed in Rabbinic literature out of respect when referring to the Lord, hence the Shekinah of the Lord speaks and performs actions thereby avoiding anthropomorphic attributes of the Lord.

28. In *Adam, Lilith and Eve*, Browning adds an ironic twist to each character. Lilith confesses her love for Adam ('If, despite this lie, he strips/ The mask from my soul with a kiss—I crawl/ His slave,—soul, body and all!'). Eve reveals that her love was for another who never arrived for the wedding, and Adam knew these secret 'passages' of their youth. In *Jocoseria*. London: Smith, Elder & Co., 1883: 53-54.

29. Siegmund Hurwitz, *Lilith—The First Eve: Historical and Psychological Aspects of the Dark Feminine*. Daimon Verlag, 1992.

30. Hurwitz, Plate 31.

31. John C.L. Gibson, *Textbook of Syrian Semitic Inscriptions*. Vol. 3 Phoenician Inscriptions including inscriptions in the mixed dialects of Arslan Tash. Oxford: Clarendon Press, 1982.

32. William Stewart McCullough, *Jewish and Mandaean Incantation Bowls in the Royal Ontario Museum*. University of Toronto Press, 1967.

33. John A. Wilson, *The Culture of Ancient Egypt*. University of Chicago Press, 1951: 156f.

34. Hurwitz.

35. Translation by Heidi M. Szpek from text in *Sipure Ben Sira bi-Yeme ha-Benayim: Mahadurah Bikortit u-Firke Mehkar*, by Eli Yasif (Jerusalem: Y.L. Magnes, 1984).

36. This adult education program was developed by the author in conjunction with Elizabeth Swados' off-broadway musical *Bible Women* and taught first at Congregation Emmanuel B'ne Jeshu-

run in Milwaukee, Wi (1996-1997). See also n. 6 "This is My Beloved and This is My Friend": Re-Imagining Eve and Adam.

37. This essay is adapted from a seven part series originally written for Themestream.com.

38. Louis Ginzberg, The Legend of the Jews. Vol. I. JPS, 1909:203.

39. Ginzberg, Vol. V. 1925:n. 122.

40. Ginzberg, Vol. I: 287; Vol. V:n. 258.

41. Ginzberg, Vol. V: n. 271.

42. John Bright, *A History of Israel.* 3rd edition. Philadelphia: Westminster Press, 1981: 69-70; 78ff.,

43. In the Isaac cycle at Gen. 26:6-11, Isaac similarly passes his wife, Rebecca, off as his sister in Gerar.

44. Ginzberg, Vol. I:221-222.

45. Geza Vermes, *The Complete Dead Sea Scrolls in English.* Penguin, 1998.

46. Ginzberg, Vol. I:238.

47. Ginzberg, Vol. V: n. 122.

48. Ginzberg, Vol. V: n. 211.

49. Ginzberg, Vol. I: 275.

50. Ginzberg, Vol. I:278.

51. Ginzberg, Vol. I:286.

52. Presented at the adult education program *Bible Women: Ancient Images and New Perspectives.* Congregation Emanuel B'ne Jeshurun. Milwaukee, WI, 1996-1997.

53. Compare the story of the Levite's concubine in Judges 19 as explored in Part III: Reclaiming, where, in a similar incident, the Levite's concubine is given to the men of the city.

54. See, for example, the New Revised Standard Version.
55. Louis Ginzberg, *The Legend of the Jews.* JPS. Vol. I (1910): 359.
56. The name for each son is tied linguistically to the explanation that follows. So, for example, Simeon (Heb. *Shim'on*) is named so "because the Lord has heard (*shm'a*) that I am hated." Both name and explanation involve the Hebrew root *shm'* "to hear."
57. Leo G. Perdue, Joseph Blenkinsopp, John J. Collins, Carol Meyers, *Families in Ancient Israel.* (Westminster/John Knox Press, 1997): 5, who comments on the numerous female characters within the book of Judges as compared to other biblical books.
58. "Judges." In *The Women's Bible Commentary.* Carol A. Newsom and Sharon H. Ringe, eds. (Louisville, Kentucky: Westminster/John Knox Press, 1992): 68.
59. For one of the earliest examinations of the textual history of Judges, see S.R. Driver, "The Origin and Structure of the Book of Judges." *JQR* 1 (1888-89): 258-270.
60. Rainer Albertz, *A History of Israelite Religion in the Old Testament Period.* Volume I: From the Beginnings to the End of the Monarchy. (Louisville, Kentucky: Westminster/John Knox Press, 1994): 99ff; William Foxwell Albright, *Yahweh and the Gods of Canaan: A Historical Analysis of Two Contrasting Faiths.* (Winona Lake, Indiana: Eisenbrauns, 1968): esp. p. 200; Erhard S. Gerstenberger, *Yahweh the Patriarch: Ancient Images of God and Feminist Theology.* (Minneapolis: Fortress Press, 1996): 73-75; Yehezkel Kaufmann, *The Religion of Israel: From Its Beginnings to the Babylonian Exile.* New York: Shocken Books, 1972): esp. pp. 138-139, 260-261; Henry Renckens, S.J., *The Religion of Israel.* (New York: Sheed and Ward, 1966): 150ff; Julius Wellhausen, *Prolegomena to the History of Ancient Israel.* (Gloucester, Mass.: Peter Smith, 1973): 228-245.

61. See especially Robert Polzin, *Moses and the Deuteronomist: A Literary Study of the Deuteronomic History. Part One: Deuteronomy, Joshua, Judges.* (New York: Seabury Press, 1993).

62. Micayehu is used in 17:1,4; Micah is used in 17:5,9,10,12,13; 18:2,3,4,13,15,18,22,23,26,27,31. See also Polzin literary treatment of Micah's story in *Moses and the Deuteronomist*, pp. 195-200.

63. This verse ends with the phrase "and now I will return it to you," over which much discussion has obtained. Most modern commentators place it at the end of Micah's words in verse two. (See note 66 below.) The ancient versions follow the Hebrew.

64. Polzin (p. 195) calls this verse the 'kernel' of Chapter 17 because it "forms a perfect summary of what precedes and follows it in the chapter."

65. Robert G. Boling, *Judges: Introduction, Translation, and Commentary.* Anchor Bible Series 6A. (Garden City, New York: Doubleday & Company, Inc.): 256.

66. See the commentaries of Boling, *Judges;* C. F. Burney, *The Book of Judges with Introduction and Notes and Notes on The Hebrew Text of the Book of Kings with an Introduction and Appendix.* (New York: KTAV Publishing House, 1970); James D. Martin, *The Book of Judges: A Commentary.* (Cambridge University Press, 1975): John L. McKenzie, S.J., *The World of the Judges* (London: Geoffrey Chapman, 1967); George Foot Moore, *A Critical and Exegetical Commentary on Judges.* The International Critical Commentary Series. (New York: Charles Schribner's Sons, 1900).

67. "Judges." In *The Women's Bible Commentary,* p. 68.

68. In Pseudo-Philo 44, Tosefta Targum, and an unknown Midrash in Rashi and Kimhi, Delilah, or erroneously Dedila, is identified in the phrase of "Micah as the son of Delilah/Dedila, the

mother of Heliu (Eli)." Her role becomes even more infamous; her son did not steal from her, but rather he possessed "one thousand pieces of gold and four wedges of melted gold and forty double pieces of silver." By taking the gold and making it into idols that will "serve as gods for you," she entices him with promises of future adoration. See James H. Charlesworth, ed., *The Old Testament Pseudepigrapha.* Volume 2. Expansions of the "Old Testament" and Legends, Wisdom and Philosophical Literature, Prayers, Psalms and Odes, Fragments of Lost Judeo-Hellenistic Works. (Garden City, New York: Doubleday & Company, Inc., 1985): pp. 357-359. The Talmud (Sanhedrin 101a) but briefly refers to Micah: [he was called] Micah, because 'he was crushed [*nkh*] in the building.' Micah's crushing refers to the legendary practice of the Egyptians forcing the Israelites to build their own children into the walls if they did not make enough bricks, hence 'Micah' and 'crushed' both derived from the root *nkh* 'to crush, smite.' Moses interceded on behalf of Micah, who related that this practice was to weed out those who were destined to be wicked. Micah was released. The proof of his wickedness was the construction of the idolatrous shrine. The Mekilta relates that Micah was also involved in building the golden calf. See Louis Ginzberg, *The Legend of the Jews.* (Philadelphia: Jewish Publication Society of America): IV, 49-50; VI, 209-210.

69. This association is based on the proximity of Micah's story immediately after the Samson and Delilah episode, and the amount of money Micah's mother possessed, 1100 pieces of silver, being the same as the payment recorded to Delilah from each of the Philistine lords in Judges 16:5.

70. Phyllis Bird notes "The Old Testament attack on foreign wives is indirect testimony to the independence and power of women within the family sphere despite the formal structures and symbols of patriarchal power. It reflects the power of influence that

wives may exert over husbands as well as the important educational role of the mother in transmitting basic religious values and wisdom essential for life. It also reflects fear of foreigners, and more particularly the foreign woman, who in Proverbs becomes the symbol for the immoral, seductive, and predatory woman, the embodiment of evil." (*Missing Persons and Mistaken Identities: Women and Gender in Ancient Israel.* Overtures to Biblical Theology. [Minneapolis: Fortress Press, 1997]: 56.)

71. *Moses and the Deuteronomist,* pp. 17-18.

72. *The World of Biblical Literature* (New York: Basic Books, 1992): 117.

73. See note 66 above.

74. *Yahweh the Patriarch,* p. 75.

75. So, for example, Micah's name both in its full form Micayehu and in the hypocoristicon Micah is a conscious albeit ironic device by the author/narrator that Yahweh *is* known; furthermore, Micah's mother blesses her son "by the Lord" (17:2) and consecrates the silver "to the Lord" (17:3). When Micah installs his non-Levitical son as priest he uses the parlance of Levitical ordination "to fill the hand." (17:5). When Micah replaces his son with a Levite, once again using the parlance of ordination, he demonstrates his knowledge of covenantal law; security is best achieved by following the precepts of Yahwism. The ephod found in Micah's shrine is certainly among the cultic accoutrements of Israelite religion, but teraphim and a molten idol belong to the realm of pagan worship (Gen. 31:19, 34-35; Exod. 20:4; 32:4). See, for example, Mircea Eliade, *A History of Religious Ideas: From Stone Age to the Eleusinian Mysteries,* Vol. I. (University of Chicago Press, 1978): 184-186; and J. Andrew Dearman, *Religion & Culture in Ancient Israel.* (Hendrickson Publishers, 1992): 142-144, for a discussion of syncretism in Israel's religion. The question that remains, however, is whether

our story indicates that not only syncretism existed but whether the idol is meant to represent the Lord himself. Commentators prefer to think of this molten image as a pedestal upon which the presence of the Lord rests, much like the bronze bulls of later Northern Kingdom shrines. Support for either assertion is subjective. That Micah and his mother were not alone in the belief that idol, ephod, teraphim and presiding Levite were acceptable cultic expressions and efficacious for future security is demonstrated by the Danites capture of these items and establishment of the cultic shrine at Dan.

76. With Ahab as with Solomon it is a foreign woman as wife that brings about apostasy. With Micah, Rehoboam, Asa and Ahaziah, mother is the culprit. Of Rehoboam, as son of Solomon who married numerous foreign wives it is not unexpected to find his mother as specifically identified as foreign. Of Micah, Asa and Ahaziah we have no such certainty.

77. See the introductory formulas of the following Judahite kings, with mothers' names in parentheses. I K 14:21 Rehoboam (Naamah the Ammonite); I K 15:4 Abijam (Maacah daughter of Abishalom); I K 15:9 Asa (Maacah daughter of Abishalom); I K 22:41 Jehoshapat (Azubah daughter of Shilhi); II K 8:16 Jehoram (no mother mentioned, but married daughter of Ahab); II K 8:25 Ahaziah (Athaliah, granddaughter of Omri); II K 11:1 Joash (Athaliah = grandmother, but under care of priest Jehoiada) /II K 12:1 Jehoash (Zibiah of Beersheba); II K 14:1 Amaziah (Jehoaddin of Jerusalem); II K 15:1 Azariah (Jecoliah of Jerusalem); II K 15:32 Jotham (Jerusha daughter of Zadok); II K 16:1 (no mother mentioned); II K 18:1 Hezekiah (Abi daughter of Zechariah); II K 21:1 Manasseh (Hephzibah); II K 21:19 Amon (Meshullemuth daughter of Haruz of Jotbah); II K 22:1 Josiah (Jedidah daughter of Adaiah of Bozkath); II K 23:31 Jehoahaz (Hamutal daughter of Jeremiah of Libnah); II K 23:36 Jehoiakim (Zebidah daughter of Pedaiah of Rumah); II K

24:8 Jehoiachin (Nehusta daughter of Elnathan of Jerusalem); II K 24:18 Zedekiah (Hamutal daughter of Jeremiah of Libnah). Ironically, in the Annals of the Kings of the North, (the region infamous for apostasy), fathers at times are noted but not mothers. The completeness of the Judahite Annal formulas (king, father, mother, length of reign and evil and good ways) may indeed reflect a proclivity on the part of the Deuteronomic Historian toward Judah. The standardized formula may also be used as device to reinforce the hereditary kingship of the South as opposed to the power by charisma and/or force in the kingship of the North.

78. In "Young Man Josiah," Lowell K. Handy, notes that the native cities of the mothers of Amon, Josiah, Jehoahaz and Jehoiachim, were located in the Galilee. With the destruction of the northern kingdom in 722BC this region would now have been under the purview of Assyria and resettled by foreignors, hence 'mother' in these cases might be deemed foreign. Paper delivered at the Midwest joint meeting of AOS/SBL/ASOR. Marquette University. Milwaukee, Wisconsin. February 15-17, 1998.

79. McKenzie, *The World of the Judges*, p. 163.

80. One need only peruse the extensive notes in the commentaries of Norman Habel *(The Book of Job*. Old Testament Library. Westminster Press, 1985) or of Marvin H. Pope (*Job: A New Translation with Introduction and Commentary*. The Anchor Bible. Doubleday & Company, 1983) to gain an understanding of the wealth of issues upon which the book of Job touches.

81. Louis Ginzberg, *The Legends of the Jews*. JPS. Vol. II. (1910): 235; Vol. V (1925): 386.

82. For the *Testament of Job*, see James H. Charlesworth, ed., *The Old Testament Pseudepigrapha*. Vol. I: Apocalyptic Literature and Testaments. Doubleday & Company, 1983: 829-868.

83. Ginzberg, *Legends*, Vol. II: 235; Vol. V: 387.

84. For details on this adult education program, entitled *Bible Women: Ancient Images and New Perspectives*, see n.15 at *What If Adam and Eve Had Been Patient?*

85. Cf. *The First Targum to Esther*. Translated and Annotated by Bernard Grossfeld. Sepher-Hermon Press, 1983.

86. On Persian history and its connection to biblical history see, for example, E. Yamauchi, *Persia and the Bible*. Baker Book House, 1990. See also J. M. Cook, *The Persian Empire*. Schoken Books, 1983, and A.T. Olmstead's classic work *History of the Persian Empire*. University of Chicago Press, 1948.

87. Louis Ginzberg, *The Legend of the Jews*. JPS. Vol. IV (1913): 373-379; Vol. VI (1928): 455-457.

88. See, for example, Athalya Brenner, ed., *A Feminist Companion to Esther, Judith and Susanna*. Sheffield: Sheffield Academic Press, 1995; Emily Cheney, *She Can Read: Feminist Reading Strategies for Biblical Narrative*. Valley Forge: Trinity Press International, 1996; Katrina J.A. Larkin, *Ruth and Esther*. Sheffield: Sheffield Academic Press, 1996; and Rivkah Lubitch, "A Feminist's Look at Esther." *Judaism* 42.4 (Fall 1993).

89. See note 6 above.

90. This story is preserved as an addition to the book of Daniel. Composed in Greek about 150BC-AD100, it is recognized as canonical (more specifically Deutero-canonical) by the Catholic Church, but not so by Judaism or Protestantism. It belongs to a group of texts called the Apocrypha ("hidden texts").

91. Cf. Deut. 17:6 "On the evidence of two or three witnesses the death sentence shall be executed."

92. Or the eight commandment. An alternate tradition reads Exod. 20:1-6 as the first commandment and divides Exod. 20:17 into the ninth and tenth commandments.

93. See Bruce Metzger, *Introduction to the Apocrypha.* Oxford University Press, 1957.

94. Consider Dorothee Solle, Joe H. Kirchberger, Herbert Haag, *Great Women of the Bible.* (Mercer University Press, 1996) for the influence the story of Susanna holds in Christian art, world literature and especially in the theatre.

95. See Francis Brown, S.R. Driver and Charles A. Briggs, *A Hebrew and English Lexicon of the Old Testament.* Oxford: Clarendon Press, 1951: 776.

96. Louis Ginzberg, *The Legends of the Jews.* JPS. Vol. I(1909): 66, 395-400; Vol. V (1925): 89, 313-14.

97. *Antiquities of the Jews.*

98. New York: Crossroad, 87.

99. The term midrash, derived from Rabbinic tradition, is used in contemporary times as a genre whose function is to retell biblical stories from a distinct perspective, incorporating additional details, while still being true to the original text.

100. "Dinah's Story: A Modern Midrash" was composed in response to an adult education course *Remembering Those Forgotten*, first taught at Congregation Emanuel B'ne Jeshurun, Mequon, WI, 1997.

101. For Rabbinic sources see above at n. 96.

102. See Phyllis Trible, *Texts of Terror: Literary-Feminist Readings of Biblical Narratives.* Fortress Press, 1984. (Dinah's story is not dealt with in detail, but other biblical stories dealing with victimized women, such as Tamar and the Levite's concubine, emphatically represent this genre.

103. For the significance of Shechem, see the previous essay, "The Rape of Dinah: Quest for Meaning."

104. The biblical text is unclear as to whether Judah's wife is name Shua or, as in v. 12, his wife is the daughter of Shua.

105. Louis Ginzberg, *The Legends of the Jews.* JPS. Vol. V(1925): 333.

106. Carol A. Newsom and Sharon H. Ringe, eds., The *Women's Bible Commentary.* Westminster/John Knox Press, 1992: 22.

107. The book of Deuteronomy records a later law (25:5-10) that allows the next of kin to refuse this duty, but it is not without the loss of honor. Consider also the book of Ruth in which the law of the Levir is also demonstrated.

108. Compare the kid/goat motif in this story to its use in Jacob-Rebecca's deception of Isaac (Gen. 27) or the blood of a kid used to stain Joseph's coat (Gen. 37). The payment for sexual favors by goat may be customary or it may be a subtle reference to these earlier deceptions.

109. Ginzberg, Vol. II: 36.

110. That the right of primogeniture is passed on to the second or a latter born son is a reoccurring theme in the book of Genesis, perhaps indicating that it is God's choice who will carry His plans forward and not this man-made law.

111. Ginzberg, Vol II: 36; V: 335.

112. Contributions to the first category, for example, include Bohmbach's (1999) analysis of Judges 19 in respect to the 'public-private construct,' private as generally accepted relates to woman's sphere and her safety—clearly our text challenges this gender stereotype. ("Conventions/Contraventions: The Meanings of Public and Private for the Judges 19 Concubine." *JSOT* 83 (1999): 83-98.) Hudson (1994) focused on anonymity in

Judges 19-21 as a literary technique that "symbolizes and epitomizes the gradual, downward spiraling disintegration that is occurring increasingly throughout the narrative until the community faces radical anarchy in chs. 17-21." ("Living in a Land of Epithets: Anonymity in Judges 19-21." *JSOT* (62): 66.) Feminist interpretation likewise has seen in this story the most horrendous period of oppression of women in the Hebrew Bible: women as possessions, as objects to be acquired and thrown aside, to be used at will without consideration would find no lower period within the panorama of biblical history.(Carol A. Newsom & Sharon H. Ringe, eds. *The Women's Bible Commentary*. Westminster/John Knox, 1991.) Janzen (1994) focuses on the demonstration of hospitality in Ch. 19: the Levite's father and the old man of Gibeah as positive models, the man of Gibeah as negative. Furthermore, that this "paradigm of behavior is broadly human" is borne in the servant's suggestion to seek hospitality in Jebus (38). (Waldemar Janzen, *Old Testament Ethics: A Paradigmatic Approach*. Westminster/John Knox, 1994.) One final example is Bal's analysis (1997) of the Levite's concubine in light of Rembrandt's etching of the concubine collapsed at the threshold at the feet of the Levite. Though depicting her death, "the moment when the woman is no longer able to speak her truth of life and death" (222), she does speak. Through the subtle shadings below her hands—shadings that cannot be shadow because the Levite and the house block her from the sun—Rembrandt suggests 'movement' (225). The concubine, "the victim at the threshold of the house, thus is forever positioned as "a liminal figure, as the embodiment of transition" (221), who "never stops dying" (222). ("A Body of Writing: Judges 19." In Athalya Brenner & Carole Fontaine, *Reading the Bible: Approaches, Methods and Strategies. A Feminist Companion to Reading the Bible*. Sheffield: Academic Press, 1997.)

113. Leiden: Brill, 1999.

114. *Kingship of God.* New York: Harper & Row, 1967.

115. Trible, *Texts of Terror: Literary-Feminist Readings of Biblical Narratives.* Overtures to Biblical Theology. Fortress Press, 1984.

116. "A Body of Writing: Judges 19." In *A Feminist Companion to Judges.* Feminist Companion to the Bible 4. Sheffield Academic Press, 1993: 208-230.

117. Rabbinic commentary, usually quite prolific for most biblical stories, is oddly scarce in the present case. Consider too that further reference to 'the crime of Gibeah' in the biblical text itself is lacking. The silence of the Rabbis is paralleled by the lack of any "sustained comment on Judges 19" from the Church Fathers. As Thompson is well to note this silence might be expected from those Church Fathers whose attention was not directed towards Judges, but the same explanation does not suffice as for example with Augustine and his students, unless "these epigones of Augustine simply refused to rush in where their master feared to tread."(John L. Thompson, *Writing the Wrongs: Women of the Old Testament among Biblical Commentators from Philo through the Reformation.* Oxford University Press, 2001: 190.) Thompson goes on to explore our story in comparison with that of Lot's daughters in Medieval Patristic and Rabbinic Sources where exegesis though present is still not extensive and tends to emphasize the MT's reading of *wattiznah* as blatantly referring to committing adultery rather than the suggested emendation to *wattiznah* "and she became angry." Moving forward to Protestant readings, the concubine as adulteress becomes even more emphatic, raising the question, why wasn't she stoned or, as the wife of a Levite, burned to death.

118. See Phyllis Trible, Texts of Terror: *Literary-Feminist Reading of Biblical Narratives.* Overtures to Biblical Theology. Philadelphia: Fortress Press, 1984: 66.

119. See Heidi M. Szpek, "Do Not Reject Your Mother's Teaching?!" The Function of Micah's Mother in Judges 17." Unpublished paper delivered at the Midwest Regional Meeting of the SBL/AAR. Marquette University. Milwaukee, WI. February 1998, published in Part Two *Rememberings* of the current collection.

120. Concubines, like Zilpah and Bilhah, who bore sons for Jacob, held a position of respect (Gen. 30:1-13); Hagar, by contrast, on bearing Ishmael became despised (Gen. 16). Other concubines were women used for sexual purposes, like Saul's concubine Rizpah (II Sam 3:7).

121. Susan Ackerman, Warrior, *Dancer, Seductress, Queen: Women in Judges and Biblical Israel.* Doubleday, 1998: 236. Understanding the Levite's concubine as secondary wife negates her "as having any ability to act independently and autonomously" (237). Ackerman's focus is clearly on the element of 'male hegemony' in this story.

122. Louis Ginzberg, *The Legends of the Jews.* JPS. VI(1928):135; Josephus, *Antiquities of the Jews.* 5.2.8.

123. Thompson explores our story in comparison with that of Lot's daughters in Medieval Patristic and Rabbinic Sources where exegesis though present is still not extensive and tends to emphasize the MT's reading of as blatantly referring to committing adultery rather than the suggested emendation to "and she became angry." Moving forward to Protestant readings, the concubine as adulteress becomes even more emphatic, raising the question, why wasn't she stoned or, as the wife of a Levite, burned to death. (*Writing the Wrongs: Women of the Old Testament among Biblical Commentators from Philo through the Reformation.* Oxford University Press, 2001:190.)

124. Trible, 67.

125. See Heidi M. Szpek, "Achsah's Story: A Metaphor of Societal Transition.," presented at the Midwest Regional Meeting of the AAR/SBL. Wheaton College. Wheaton, IL. February 1997, forthcoming in Andrews University Seminary Studies.

126. *Rembrandt Bible Drawings: 60 Works by* Rembrandt van Rijn. New York: Dover Publications, Inc., 1979.

127. No less than a month later, in preparing this paper, I chanced upon another etching by Rembrandt. Searching the stacks of the Suzzallo & Allen Library at the University of Washington for another volume my attention was drawn to another volume. Within I found yet another article expounding Marcel Proust's retelling of the Levite's Concubine—a retelling that incidentally caused him to be run out of town! Within this analysis an etching by Rembrandt appeared, once again turning to this tale of terror. This later etching, entitled *The Levite Finds his Wife in the Morning* (1655), depicted that most horrendous moment when the Levite discovers the collapsed body of his concubine on the doorsteps of the old man of Gibeah's house.

128. Louis Ginzberg, *The Legends of the Jews*. JPS. V(1925): 258.

129. **Noah's wife** is named Naamah 'pleasant one' in Rabbinic tradition and is believed to be the daughter of Enosh or Enoch (Gen. 5:6,9,18,21). She was considered the only pious woman of her generation and her good deeds equaled Noah's. She does not speak a word in the text; we are simply told she went with Noah, his sons and their wives (Gen. 6:18; 7:13; 8:16,18). Without hesitation we assume she supported Noah when the Lord commanded him to build an ark. (Gen. 6:5-9:19)

Sarah, the wife of Abraham, is the first Matriarch. Selflessly she journeyed with Abraham, her husband, from her homeland in Ur of the Chaldees throughout the Ancient Near East. She bore the burden of barrenness until age 90 when through divine intervention she bore Isaac. She was a woman devoted to her husband, her son and to God, yet her voice rang out when her only son Isaac was endangered. (Gen. 11:27-Ch. 23)

Rebekah, wife of Isaac, is the second Matriarch. Her life is reminiscent of Sarah, for she, too, left her homeland of Paddan-aram in Northern Mesopotamia to become Isaac's wife, sight unseen. She, too, suffered barrenness, but unlike Sarah, divine intervention came soon. She bore twins, Esau and Jacob. Her devotion turned toward Jacob, God's choice through whom His people would continue. It was Rebekah who consoled Isaac who for three years mourned the loss of his mother Sarah. (Gen. 24-27)

Leah, first wife of Jacob, is the third Matriarch. In *Leah of 'Dim' Eyes,* I wrote of how she was unloved by her husband, because her younger sister Rachel was first betrothed and shared a mutual love with Jacob. Her father Laban switched sisters at the wedding ceremony, thus elder Leah married before Rachel. But Leah's legacy came with the six sons and one daughter she bore for Jacob, among whom one stands most regal, Judah, from whom the Davidic line is descended. (Gen. 29-33)

Rachel, second wife of Jacob, younger sister of Leah, is the fourth Matriarch. She first beheld and fell in love with Jacob. His feelings were mutual. When her father, Laban, tricked Jacob into first marrying her sister Leah, she could not contest his deception for the custom was older daughter before younger. Like the matriarchs Sarah and Rebekah, Rachel, too, was barren. It was only after her sister had bore four sons that Rachel gave her handmaid to Jacob to bear sons on her behalf. Two sons were born: Dan and Naphtali. In turn Leah (who had ceased bearing) gave her handmaid Zilpah to Jacob, who also bore two sons: Gad and Asher. Leah herself bore two more sons and a daughter. And finally God remembered Rachel and she bore Joseph. Joseph became the beloved of Jacob. Though sold into slavery by his brothers out of jealousy, it is Joseph who will save his family when famine strikes Canaan. Rachel will bear another son for Jacob, Benjamin, but she will die in childbirth. (Gen. 29-33)

Bithiah, Moses' foster mother, is the daughter of the Pharaoh of Egypt. Her Egyptian name was Thermutis. Bithiah is the name given to her in Rabbinic tradition by God, meaning "daughter of the Lord." (Ginzberg, *Legends*, Vol. V (1925): 398). It was Bithiah who adopted baby Moses when his mother set him adrift on the Nile. At that time the Hebrew people were under great persecution and though she recognized him as a Hebrew (because he was circumcised), she took him in at great danger to herself and raised him as her own. (Exod. 2)

Jochebed is Moses' birth mother; both she and her husband were of the Levitic (priestly) line. The name Jochebed is found in Exodus 6:20. At the time she bore Moses, Pharaoh had ordered that all Hebrew baby boys be thrown into the Nile out of fear for the ever- increasing population and power of the Hebrews. Jochebed hid baby Moses for three months and, realizing this was no longer feasible, she gave up her child that he might be saved. Fate and/or divine intervention brought Jochebed to serve as nursemaid to Moses! (Exod. 2)

Miriam was Moses' sister. It was she who watched that baby Moses safely reached Pharaoh's daughter after he was set afloat in a basket on the Nile. It was Miriam who offered to find a nursemaid for Pharaoh's daughter, the nursemaid being none other than their mother. Miriam went on to be a leader among women; she is a called a prophetess (Exod. 15:20). Rabbinic tradition records that while she lived a well, Miriam's well, would always provide for the Israelites in the wilderness (Ginzberg, *Legends*, Vol. I: (1909): 265). At her death, there was no water for the congregation (Numb. 20:1-2; see also Exod. 2; 15:20-21; Numb. 12)

Hannah, greatly beloved wife of Elkanah, was the mother of the greatest judge Samuel. She, too, suffered from barrenness, but because of her great devotion and prayers, the Lord intervened and she conceived. Even before she conceived she vowed that if the Lord remembered her she would dedicate her child as a nazir, a special servant of God who did not partake in wine, intoxicants or cut his hair. He would be totally devoted to the Lord. Hannah kept her promise. When Samuel had been weaned she brought him to Shiloh, to the high priest Eli, to be trained to minister to the Lord. (I Samuel 1-2)

Jael, wife of Heber the Kenite, took a tent peg to the head of Sisera, mighty general of King Jabin of Canaan who had been oppressing Israel for twenty years. It was the judge Deborah who had lead the Israelite's general Barak to the battle, but it was Jael who brought down the mighty Sisera. (Judges 4-5)

The widow of Zarephath appears in I Kings 17, within the cycle of stories about the prophet Elijah. In this story the prophet asks her to bring him a little water and a morsel of bread. She was very poor, preparing to use the last of her supplies to feed her son and herself, after which she believed they would die. But Elijah encouraged her use the last of her food to nourish him, noting that the jar of meal and jar of oil will not fail. She believed and it was so. When her son took ill and died, however, she blamed Elijah. Elijah revived the boy and her belief increased manifold in this man of God. Rabbinic tradition teaches that the widow of Zarephath was instrumental in softening the inflexibility of the prophet Elijah and that her son was the prophet Jonah (Ginzberg, *Legends*, Vol. VI (1928): 351).

Naomi, wife of Elimelech, followed her husband with her two sons from Bethlehem of Judah to the non-Israelite country of

Moab because famine had struck their land. Her husband died, her sons married Moabite women and they died without heirs. Naomi was left in Moab with no kin save two Moabite daughters-laws. Determining her salvation was in Bethlehem, she returned with one daughter-in-law, Ruth (see below), traveling alone through the treacherous Judean wilderness to Bethlehem of Judah. Once in Bethlehem she needed to provide for herself and her daughter-in-law, Ruth the Moabite. And she did, thereby maintaining the inheritance of her husband's lineage. (Book of Ruth)

Rahab was the harlot who hid two Israelite spies as they spied out Jericho and the land of Canaan just prior to the conquest of the Holy Land (Josh. 2). Though we might question her designation as an *'eshet hayil* by virtue of her profession, she did hide the spies, saving them, while jeopardizing the lives of her family and herself. When Joshua and Israel attacked Jericho (Josh. 6), she and her family were spared by hanging a crimson cord from her window—a pre-established signal of her earlier assistance. Legend has it that on seeing the Israelites she gave up her immoral life and converted, became Joshua's wife and the ancestress of eight prophets (including Jeremiah) and the prophetess Huldah.

Bath-sheba was the wife of Uriah the Hittite, whom David sent into the front lines of battle after having an affair and impregnating her. She became David's second wife. The child of their adulterous relationship died, but their next child became the famed Solomon of Israel. (2 Sam. 11-12)

Michal, daughter of Saul (first king of Israel), sister of Jonathan, the beloved friend of David, became David's first wife. From David's perspective, their marriage may have been a political maneuver, but Michal truly loved David (1 Sam. 18:20). Michal's love grew for David, as did the people of Israel's, much to King Saul's dismay. Though Michal will later despise David for his dance of victory (2 Sam. 6:16) and will never bear his child (2 Sam. 6:23), it is Michal who saved David, the greatest king of Israel, from her father Saul's soldiers (1 Sam. 18:23).

Hazlelponith, was the mother of Samson, the judge known for his great strength, a passion for Philistine women (Delilah), and for fighting against the Philistines who had oppressed Israel for forty years (Judg. 13:1). Like Sarah, Rebekah, Rachel, Hannah, she, too, was barren until God's intervention. Her son was destined to be a *nazir* like Samuel and in anticipation she steadfastly followed the words of the angel of annunciation, "Now be careful not to drink wine or strong drink, or to eat anything unclean for you shall conceive and bear a son" (Judg. 13:4-5). When her husband Manoah received this news from an angelic messenger, it was Hazlelponith who calmed his fears that having seen God they would die. Her name, Hazlelponith, is not found in the biblical text, but derives from Rabbinic literature.

Elisheba is a woman deemed prestigious because her husband, Aaron, was the high priest of the Israelites; her brother-in-law Moses was their leader; her son, Eleazer was the head of the priests, her grandson and brother were also prominent. Her sons Nadab and Abihu, however, offered unholy fire before the Lord and were consumed by heavenly fire. Her name is noted in Exod. 6:23. While Jochebed and Miriam are often connected with Shiphrah and Puah, the Hebrew midwives (Exod. 1:15), other Rabbinic traditions relate that Elisheba was Puah (Ginzberg, *Legends*, Vol. V (1925): 393). Together with Shiphrah they not only assisted as midwives, but also provided for any needs of the mother. It was through their efforts that the Hebrews continued to be fruitful despite Pharaoh's command to kill all the new-born babies.

Serah is the daughter of Asher, second son of Leah's handmaid Zilpah and Jacob. According to one Rabbinic tradition Serah was skilled with the harp and song. Her uncles, fearing their father's reprisal, sent Serah to bring the news to her grandfather Jacob that Joseph was alive, living well in Egypt (Ginzberg, Legends Vol. V (1925): 356, 369).

The wife of Obadiah, the prophet, who declared his condemnation of the wicked country of Edom (see the book of Obadiah), is connected in Rabbinic and Christian circles with the widow in 2 Kings 4:1-7. We find her impoverished, with her two children about to be sold to a creditor, but she had one jar of oil. Along came the prophet Elisha who performed a miracle; she borrowed numerous empty vessels from her neighbors and the vessels became filled from her one jar. She sold the oil, paid her debts and supported her children and herself throughout their lives. Elisha had helped her because she had supported her husband when he used their fortune, as well as borrowed money, to support the prophets who were in hiding from the wicked King Ahab (Ginzberg, Legends, Vol. IV: (1913): 240-41).

The **Shunnamite woman** was a wealthy woman who provided food and lodging for the prophet Elisha whenever he passed through her village. She did this of her own free will. In return Elisha foretold that she who had been childless would bear a son. And she did, but later when the child grew older he died from a brain aneurysm. Like his mentor Elijah, Elisha brought the child back to life. (2 Kings 4:8-37)

Ruth, the Moabite, married Mahlon, son of Elimelech and Naomi when they sojourned in her native land of Moab. Her father-in-law died, then her husband and brother-in-law, but Ruth, now a widow, clung to her mother-in-law Naomi, unlike her sister-in-law Orphah. Ruth did not return to her father's house, but traveled with Naomi back to Bethlehem of Judah. She willingly followed Naomi, accepted Naomi's home, people and God. Together the two women saw that the line of Elimelech would not die out. Through their machinations Ruth married Boaz, a next-of-kin, and bore a son, Obed, the grandfather of King David.

Esther, a Jewish maiden, lived in Susa of Persia. After the disposition of the reigning Queen Vashti and a 'beauty contest' to search for a new queen, Esther became their Queen. She came to the throne, marrying a non-Jew, not in a quest for power, but to save her people. A certain high-ranking official named Haman had maneuvered the king into passing a decree to annihilate all the Jews in his kingdom. Esther did not convince the king to rescind the degree—this would be contrary Persian custom—but she convinced him to pass a new degree that the Jews be allowed to defend themselves. And they did (Book of Esther).

130. *A Guide to Old Kona*. Kona Historical Society. Kalukalu, Kona, 1998: 63-64.

0-595-24906-X

Printed in the United Kingdom
by Lightning Source UK Ltd.
102637UKS00001B/231